ADVANCE PRAISE FOR

Strong Community Service Learning

"This is a wonderful resource for practitioners that anchors Community Service Learning in its philosophical and historical roots. Reflection is the heart of service learning. Eric C. Sheffield explores the ways it links emotion and intellect to create powerful transformative experiences for students."

Janet Eyler, Co-Author,
A Practitioner's Guide to Reflection in Service-Learning: Student Voices and Reflections *and* Where's the Learning in Service-Learning?

"This important book is a call for community in a time of accelerating barbarism. It is a cry for education as a human right and a pillar of democracy against all the powerful voices now aligned with an arid view of education as nothing more than preparation for a brutal war—all against all—in which we can only survive if we beat the Chinese or the Indians or some future designated Other into submission. In that war I'll choose to be a conscientious objector. Eric C. Sheffield shows me how."

William Ayers, Author,
To Teach: The Journey, in Comics *and* Teaching Toward Freedom

"Through this thoughtful and rich analysis of the historical, philosophical, and epistemological underpinnings of Community Service Learning, Eric C. Sheffield helps us understand the vital importance of high quality practice and the potential of 'strong' Community Service Learning to fulfill the promise of social change."

Andrew Furco,
Associate Vice President for Public Engagement,
University of Minnesota, Twin Cities

"Through critical analysis of current service-learning, Eric C. Sheffield presents a vision of strong service-learning that goes beyond service or charity that sustains current social inequities. This passionately argued book is deeply grounded in important philosophical traditions that challenge educators and students to make a difference in the social order. A must read for anyone concerned about quality in service-learning and the role of schools in the creation of a more just social order."

Dwight E. Giles Jr., Co-Author,
Where's the Learning in Service-Learning?

"Eric C. Sheffield's brief for Community Service Learning is a model for philosophic thinking: embedded in a story of a real problem, clarifying meanings, analyzing relationships, and proposing solutions to be tried—all within the context of democratic values and practices and historical awareness. It is a clear and consistent argument that should be the last word on this good idea. All that remains is to put it into practice."

Robert R. Sherman, Emeritus,
University of Florida

Strong Community Service Learning

Adolescent Cultures, School & Society

Joseph L. DeVitis & Linda Irwin-DeVitis

GENERAL EDITORS

Vol. 53

The Adolescent Cultures, School & Society series
is part of the Peter Lang Education list.
Every volume is peer reviewed and meets
the highest quality standards for content and production.

PETER LANG
New York • Washington, D.C./Baltimore • Bern
Frankfurt • Berlin • Brussels • Vienna • Oxford

Eric C. Sheffield

Strong **Community Service Learning**

Philosophical Perspectives

PETER LANG
New York • Washington, D.C./Baltimore • Bern
Frankfurt • Berlin • Brussels • Vienna • Oxford

Library of Congress Cataloging-in-Publication Data

Sheffield, Eric C.
Strong community service learning: philosophical perspectives /
Eric C. Sheffield.
p. cm. — (Adolescent cultures, school and society; v. 53)
Includes bibliographical references and index.
1. Teachers—Training of—Cross-cultural studies.
2. Teachers—In-service training—Cross-cultural studies. I. Title.
LB1707.S44   370.71'1—dc22   2011010251
ISBN 978-1-4331-1244-7 (hardcover)
ISBN 978-1-4331-1243-0 (paperback)
ISSN 1091-1464

Bibliographic information published by **Die Deutsche Nationalbibliothek**.
Die Deutsche Nationalbibliothek lists this publication in the "Deutsche
Nationalbibliografie"; detailed bibliographic data is available
on the Internet at http://dnb.d-nb.de/.

The paper in this book meets the guidelines for permanence and durability
of the Committee on Production Guidelines for Book Longevity
of the Council of Library Resources.

© 2011 Peter Lang Publishing, Inc., New York
29 Broadway, 18th floor, New York, NY 10006
www.peterlang.com

All rights reserved.
Reprint or reproduction, even partially, in all forms such as microfilm,
xerography, microfiche, microcard, and offset strictly prohibited.

Printed in the United States of America

For Stefan, Ezra, Dana, Mom and Dad;
and in loving memory of April.

Contents

Foreword

Eric Sheffield's interesting book on community service learning (CSL) is especially timely in today's educational climate. We are immersed in a sea of money-talk: all young people should go to college in order to make more money; the nation needs more college graduates in order to compete in the world economy. The focus is on money and competition. High school students in "good" schools compete vigorously for high grades, recognition in extracurricular activities, and admission to prestigious colleges. Instead of sharing information with their peers, some students actually withhold it so that they can maintain a competitive edge.

In the adult world, the focus on money sharpens as people compete for jobs that will enable them to pay off their student loans and climb the economic ladder. There is little time to participate in the local community. In academia, there is growing interest in cosmopolitanism—an attitude that embraces the whole world as a center for citizenship. Although this attitude is commendable, it too is sometimes accompanied by a diminished interest in the local community.

CSL, as described by Sheffield, contributes to a reconciliation of local and global commitment. Students engaged in CSL learn how to interact with local strangers and to work cooperatively to solve problems and build community in the process. The skills and attitudes gained in this work can then be applied in wider circles.

There is also a powerful intellectual dimension in CSL. Too often today we suppose that all students must be enrolled in algebra, physics, and classic literature if they are to grow intellectually. Sheffield, following William Heard Kilpatrick, notes that participants in CSL are fully engaged in purposing, planning, executing, and judging (evaluating). The intellectual demands are both challenging and practical; they arise in a real social world and are not contrived.

As the comprehensive high school weakens and gives way to a single-track curriculum or to magnet and special vocational schools, it becomes harder for the school to maintain its 20th-century role as a builder of democracy. Where, formerly, young people from a variety of curricular programs would come together to participate in athletics, clubs, artistic activities, and school government, today's students are often forced into one academic curriculum or separated into different schools. CSL provides an opportunity to invigorate democracy both within the school and in the outside community.

Sheffield makes an interesting distinction between "weak" and "strong" CSL. The weak version, he writes, is compatible with an orientation toward reform; it is "democratic in its means" and its aim "is the extension of democratic habits of action from and through schools into the broader community." It falls a bit short of strong CSL, he says, in that it is not aimed directly at building a new social order. Readers may react to this as I have. In today's educational world, "weak" CSL—if enacted—is quite wonderful. It demands reflective deliberation, social activism, nondiscrimination, and nonrepression. Continued, energetic commitment to this approach may well lead eventually and naturally to the strong CSL that Sheffield envisions. Let's hope policymakers listen and support CSL.

Nel Noddings
Stanford University

Preface

At the end of *The Protestant Ethic and The Spirit of Capitalism*, Max Weber portrays a human experience ineluctably ensnared within the "iron cage of capitalism. Lives, according to Weber, have become bound by birth to the technical and economic conditions of machine-age production. Weber's scant portrayal of life inside this "iron cage" is coupled with only a brief foretelling of what life might be like inside here in the future.

> No one knows who will live in this cage in the future, or whether at the end of this tremendous development entirely new prophets will arise, or there will be a great rebirth of old ideas and ideals, or, if neither, mechanized petrification, embellished with a sort of convulsive self-importance. For the last stage of this cultural development, it might well be truly said: 'Specialists without spirit, sensualists without heart, this nullity imagines that it has attained a level of civilization never before achieved.'"[1]

One hundred years have passed since the publication of Weber's text, and we now stand witness to much of the mechanized deadness in experience that he anticipated. It seems that the tenets of the Enlightenment which promised to free humankind from despotic rulers, dogmatic priests, and binding traditions have become the material out of which a more insidious set of fetters has emerged to shackle human life. The idea that morally individuals should be free and equal in the pursuit of happiness as each sees fit as long as this pursuit somehow contributes to the well-being of others has become bastardized to mean each individual's right and responsibility to pursue happiness defined solely in terms of material goods. Buying goods has become the everyday expression of self-realization and the primary mode of social interaction. Bodies have been disciplined, routinized, and organized into a regime of profit production. Souls have been habituated, ruled and regulated, administered and measured according to the high principle of wealth accumulation. Desires, wants, drives for personal fulfillment and happiness are concocted, marketed, and satisfied through the consumption of goods. The moral ideal of citizenship is one based upon a shared commitment to producing the greatest range of stuff for the greatest number of people. It is not surprising, then, that character and individual well-being often are measured in terms of material accumulated, brands, and personal net-worth. "Social excellence" now signifies higher standards of living and levels of consumption quantitatively noted. We exist confidently in the belief that our intelligence, wit, and effort will force nature to yield up her secrets such that we may construct tools and instruments to induce her further to yield up yet more secrets for our profit. The machinery, gadgets, and instruments that seem to give value to our experience serve as evidence to confirm how right we are in our faith and to mitigate against the ill effects of fallible human judgment, particularly the irrationality and irresponsibility of thinking that there is life outside of this cage. Furthermore, we are secure in the idea that our technology, as the embodiment of nature's laws, can discipline out all that is erratic and uncertain in human behavior and thus align it to be more efficient and exact in the grand production of the trade-marked Good Life.

It should not be news, then, to those reading this text that public schools have served—at least in part—as one of the instruments in the regulation of social and political sentiment required by a capitalist system. By the 1920s, volume, efficiency, and control became the mantra chanted by school bureaucrats and the serial casting of human beings into productive economic forms became the practical aim of schooling. How this business model came to be hegemonic in and through public schooling is a complex, richly-textured tale well-documented and better told by educational historians. However, the upshot seems clear. Our prevailing conception of schooling has produced generations of youth that are easily hoodwinked, emotionally reactionary, and frustrated in their struggle to shed their commodified skins. At least as far as schooling is concerned, we have sent them into the world without well-formed habits of mind and human connection necessary to engage in meaningful existential questioning and organic soul making. As Cornel West puts it in *Democracy Matters*, young people "long for emerging visions worthy of pursuit and sacrifice that will situate their emaciated souls in a story bigger than themselves and locate their inflated egos (that only conceal deep insecurities and anxieties) in a narrative grander than themselves."[2]

In a time at which our public schools triumphantly portray human becoming in terms of that which can be neatly packaged and conveniently consumed, telling a story in which homo economicus is not the protagonist may seem ridiculously anachronistic to some. However, my long time friend Eric Sheffield draws on an ancient story of love in which the human embrace of hazard, uncertainty, and risk serves as the means by which the infinite possibilities of the soul are birthed and transcend the "iron cage."

As Diotima explains to Socrates in Plato's *Symposium*, love is a daimon, an intermediary between heaven and earth. Seizing upon this notion of love as it descends through American Pragmatism, Sheffield, although not in these exact terms, depicts shared practice as a daimon. Shared practices are the fluid forms of approaching and embracing the uncertain and dangerous in experience. They are the means by which we develop skill and knowledge of ourselves with the world. They embody ideals, standards of excellence, virtues, and principals. Shared practices induce wonder, openness, sympathy, a will to share, wholehearted attention, thoughtfulness, and faith. As daimons, shared practices lead us to a religious appreciation of experience, to a divine sense of our connection with others who animate the universal, the immortal, and by virtue of such understanding, "we are carried beyond ourselves to find ourselves."[3] Sheffield's work here is an admirable attempt to recover a sense of educational grace in an otherwise spiritually barren educational landscape.

Randy Hewitt
University of Central Florida

Acknowledgments

I first want to acknowledge two people who have historically impacted my thinking, continue to do so, and without whom the ideas presented in this book would never have been developed: Robert R. Sherman and Randy Hewitt. Dr. Sherman has been a mentor, friend, and colleague for many years now and it was "Rob" (as his students ultimately come to know him) who carefully guided me to and then through the philosophy of pragmatism. Randy was one of Rob's students as well. He was also a year or two ahead of me, helping me with the dissertation "process" and was invaluable in the considering of ideas and how they might be put into practice. As time passed, Randy became and remains one of my dearest friends. I am happy that you will find both Rob and Randy's influence throughout.

Thanks to the Interlachen High School community: I learned more about living in my fourteen years there than in any period of my life—and a special thanks to Coach Jack Williams and the Ehrhardt clan for enriching my life in ways I never expected from a career teaching high school English.

I also would be remiss in not mentioning my colleague here at Missouri State University, Steven P. Jones. Steve has encouraged me to approach my life as a university professor with nothing less than full speed ahead. His brainchild, the Academy for Educational Studies, has also provided me professional, intellectual, and social opportunities that I never dreamed would be availed me. I want to thank another Missouri State colleague, Roger Sell, who, in passing one day, suggested that this should be a book. Many thanks also to Joe DeVitis, Peter Lang series editor, for his revision suggestions, which have made this a stronger book.

Finally, I owe a heartfelt debt of gratitude to my dear friend and colleague, Jessica Heybach. I suspect Jessica does not realize how she impacted my thinking throughout the writing of this book. She listened to my ideas, suggested things to read, pondered with me, and at times made suggestions for change and redirection. She patiently pushed me to look at the ideas contained herein from different perspectives. She also picked me up, brushed me off, and got me through the various crises of confidence I experienced during the writing of this book. Thanks Jess. I'm not sure I would have made it through this without you cheering me on.

CHAPTER ONE

My CSL Story

Reading the work of John Dewey in the early days of my graduate studies, I was convinced of philosophy's value as a research paradigm sourced in lived experience. Mr. Dewey also convinced me that scholarly work, particularly philosophical work, has little or no value if it does not suggest practical ways to improve lived experience; in not making lived experience "better," philosophy fails to meet the criterion of an important human social practice. This project itself comes from my own lived experience—it has a story—and this project has philosophically grounded "doable" suggestions for improving that story—but more on that story momentarily.

I have three core aims in writing this book. First, there is its stated aim: I hope to provide some sorely needed philosophical perspective that can ground community service learning conceptually/philosophically, and in so doing suggest practical ways that CSL projects can be improved. Second, I hope to convince anyone who has an interest in pursuing or improving CSL that its full potential exists in what I will call "strong" CSL. The "weak" version of it, as it most often exists today, does have some value as an academically democratic endeavor; however, in constructing the strong version later in the book, I make the case that incorporating a rather virulent critical perspective into CSL can make it more "transformative" for individuals, schools, and whole communities. My third aim is much more "big picture," as I explain below.

I have over the last several years, particularly since leaving the world of secondary public schooling, noticed an understandable reticence among practicing and pre-service teachers (my current students) when I ask them to read scholarship generally described as philosophical. I say understandable because, quite honestly, much of what philosophers of education "do" rings hollow relative to the lived experiences of real teachers and real students who toil in (and out) of real American classrooms. I remember feeling much the same way, particularly in the early years of my high school teaching career.

On the other hand, I have come to believe that philosophical work in education, when done with an eye for improving actual school policy and practice, has immense practical value. There are indeed problems in the messy, "real" world of American classrooms that can be eased, if not completely corrected, by analyzing, recla- rifying, and reapplying the conceptual underpinnings that drive educational practice. In its continual conceptual analysis of prac- tice, I believe diligent practical philosophy has the potential to fix many of our contemporary school ills—ills so often lamented by teachers, students, politicians, policymakers, parents, and citizens alike. My third aim, then, is to convince you of philosophy's prac- tical value in improving educational practices such as CSL.

With that in mind, I want to assure you that in these pages you will not find an irrelevant set of philosophical musings from an ivory-towered academic who has no practical understanding of the messiness of American classrooms. As I said, there is a story here and that story comes out of my fourteen years teaching high school English in an impoverished community in north-central Florida where I tried out the CSL pedagogy but with only limited success. I also want to assure you that in advocating for the strong version of CSL later in the book—which I believe can provide the means to analyze institutional oppression and suggest communal action that can ease or eliminate that oppression—I will endeavor to keep it local, practical, and, I hope, helpful, rather than abstractly dis- connected from actual school experience.

And so, my story...

In my third year of teaching, a politically and socially active student by the name of April Ehrhardt approached me with an idea and a request: "I would like to start an environmental service club. Would you be its sponsor?" My response was "absolutely." It was not long before the Society for Environmentally Conscientious Students (SECS) was born, actively promoting environmental ste- wardship through a school-wide recycling program, an environ- mental awareness fair, an adopted piece of highway adjacent to the school, and, importantly for the present discussion, a partner- ship with a local state park. (The acronym for the organization, SECS, was a clever ploy by the founding students who could, with wry humor, invite fellow students to join "SECS.")

As the years passed, SECS grew, and impressively so. At its height, a passerby might see as many as 40 students early on a Saturday morning walking the highway, picking up trash. These were some very impressive young people indeed, particularly given that this was *before* community service was a graduation requirement. The partnership with the local state park, part of a larger statewide initiative called PARKnership, also became more vibrant as time went on and led to suggestions by both park and school personnel that it might grow into something educationally powerful—if only there were resources available. Enter the federal service-learning grant program.

I sat down with park personnel and crafted a grant proposal most essentially based on their perceived park needs, relying little on any real understanding of CSL, and much on that age-old grant-writing technique: use all the right buzzwords (in this case, "reflection," "community," "collaboration," "mutual service," and so on). We sent off the proposal suspecting that our chances of being supported were slim. Several months later, however, we received word that we had been awarded the grant.

The grant monies supported three PARKnership projects: the construction of a boardwalk that led down into a beautiful, though somewhat inaccessible ravine; the planting of a butterfly garden; and, because even the boardwalk did not allow for complete access to the ravine (the heart of the park), the creation of a video "tour" that presented the flora, the fauna, and the history of the park. Aside from the students and myself, I recruited a biology teacher, an art teacher, the shop teacher, the agriculture teacher, the district media guru, the park rangers, and Coach Jack Williams, the heart and soul of the school community.

As the projects evolved, I was amazed at what I saw: research into the butterflies of the region as well as the native plants that would attract the butterflies; the construction of a display kiosk; the installation of an irrigation system; the study of soil best suited for growing the butterfly-attracting plants; a hand-painted butterfly identification chart (probably the most impressive student-made piece of art I have ever witnessed); the design and construction of a boardwalk; the production of a butterfly garden brochure; the writing of a video script based on both environmental and historical research; the filming and editing of raw video subsequently fused with a student-written narrative that resulted

in an impressive visual presentation of the park. Imagine my joy
in seeing these kinds of classroom academics put to use improving
an important community resource via a community effort among
students, teachers, and park rangers! However, that joy came
crashing down as the projects came to an end.

Part of the grant requirement was a project-ending celebration
and a "reflective" activity that would allow students to explore and
explain what they learned from the various projects. The celebration took place on the park grounds and the reflective activity involved open-ended written reflections on the students' experiences
during the projects. When I perused the responses, I felt a sinking
feeling in my gut as I read over and over again that students most
enjoyed "getting out of the school" for part of the day "to go have
fun with friends" in the park. Missing was just about everything I
expected to read: commentary on the experiential value of academics; mention of a robust belief in community service; descriptions of
a new-found feeling of ownership toward the park; the champion-
ing of environmental stewardship. There was not even significant
mention of the relationships I thought they had built while working side by side with the park personnel—yes, there was a smat-
tering of such comments, but something was terribly wrong.

John Dewey suggests that we initially realize we have a problem emotionally and physically—we feel that something is amiss.
I agree, particularly so in this case. He also suggests that emotion
of this sort is an integral part of truly reflective, truly critical, truly philosophical thought and action. Emotion is the catalyst to
thought, which leads to acting in the name of recovering one's lost
emotional equilibrium. I was incredibly disturbed by this experience. The sinking feeling I experienced upon reading those student reflections lead me on my first real philosophical journey. It
occurred just as I returned to graduate school amidst a sea of reading and inquiry. This book is the result of that journey.

What I discovered in my journey is that there is precious little
philosophical grounding for CSL, and the little that does exist consists of some rather disconnected suggestions that CSL is based on
generally progressive notions of education (in fact, it is) found in
the work of numerous early-20th-century educational thinkers.
More contemporary CSL scholarship tends toward "how-to" suggestions, traditional research on its educational outcomes, or increasingly in the work of critical theorists—none of which provides

a comprehensively clear and practical conceptual/philosophical basis for CSL. This book is an attempt to construct, clarify, and connect the philosophical dots that can support vibrant "educative" CSL projects, particularly in P–12 schools.

The structure of the book is simple: Chapter Two is a defense of practical philosophy as a viable research method—one that I believe all teachers should and can make use of to create more vibrant educative experiences. It is unapologetically pragmatic, plain, and simple, as I believe most philosophical work can be. Chapter Three provides a brief discussion of the conceptual history of CSL, because it's important to understand how far CSL has come so that we might envision where it can go. Chapter Four takes up the issue of what I hoped to find but didn't in the PARK-nership student reflections: the educational aims that might be expected from a clear understanding of CSL. This chapter sets out the aims of CSL via a categorical/philosophical structure that foreshadows the conceptual chapters that follow it.

Chapters Five through Eight are organized around the core conceptual underpinnings of CSL: community, service, experiential learning, and reflection—my goal being to clarify and connect these core conceptions philosophically, with each chapter culminating in a discussion of its practical implications. In Chapters Nine and Ten, I take up more "external" issues of CSL. I suggest a distinction between a "weak" and "strong" conception of CSL: the former informed by a classically mundane understanding of democratic education; the latter by a more radical one. Finally, I conclude in Chapter Eleven with some suggestions as to where those of us engaged in the work of encouraging and growing the practice of CSL might look to improve the story, including a critical critique of my own PARKnership experience.

Before getting to the work, I should explain that I am a firm believer that there really are not that many new ideas under the sun; we certainly stand on the shoulders of relatively taller and shorter historic giants. That being the case, I rely heavily on those historic giants and hope to bring together in a single volume a philosophically sound and practically oriented foundation for promoting and growing a truly transformative pedagogy of emotional, academic, experiential and activist growth. We can make the CSL story continually better. I hope you agree.

CHAPTER TWO

Making the Case for Philosophy

Introduction

As described in Chapter One, this project has three aims: first, the title-stated aim of bringing philosophical perspective to the practice of community service learning; second, suggesting that a critically strong conception for CSL might be constructed to meet its full potential; and third, making the case that philosophical work is a practical research endeavor, one that I believe all educators would be well served in pursuing. This second chapter is my one and only direct appeal to convince you of the latter; the remaining chapters illustrate how practical philosophical work can improve CSL, and by extension, other contemporary educational stories.[1]

I also want to be clear that I come at this CSL clarifying project from a particular philosophical tradition—one that is essentially American—and one that fits my understanding of philosophy as a practical endeavor. That tradition is variously known as pragmatism, instrumentalism, social reconstructionism, or progressivism. It is the tradition born out of the thought of William James, put into a logic by C.S. Peirce, brought to maturity by John Dewey, somewhat radicalized by George Counts and adopted, albeit with some rather clumsy language, by critical theorists. I think that coming at practical educational endeavors such as CSL from this tradition simply makes good sense for several reasons.

First, the pragmatic tradition takes as its starting point human "lived" experience and how conceptual understandings play out in that experience; in my case, an experience in a living, breathing, messy, impoverished high school in north-central Florida where I tried out the CSL pedagogy. Second, and as a pragmatic matter, I see no reason to reinvent the proverbial conceptual wheel. As I have argued elsewhere, philosophical work is not often a completely creative endeavor (it is rare indeed that a Plato, Aristotle, James, Kierkegaard, or Wittgenstein comes along to create a new philosophical paradigm). Most of the philosophical pieces needed to improve the CSL story already exist. [2] The chore then is "simply" one of philosophical reminding via the reclarification, reconstruction, and reapplication of those existing concepts to CSL practice—and that, I believe, is an endeavor indicative of pragmatism. Finally, a philosophically pragmatic approach makes sense given that the CSL concept and its resulting practice come directly out of the thinking of progressive educators such as John Dewey, W.H. Kilpatrick, and Paul Hanna. In the next chapter, I briefly take up some of the pragmatic history of CSL.

However, before "philosophizing" the particular story of CSL, I will lay out the case for seeing philosophy as a useful, practical, and essential educational research endeavor—one that can bring some clarity to CSL and other important pedagogies.

Philosophy as a Social Practice

As with all enduring human enterprises, philosophical endeavors are a part of the social experience that exists when one is born and that will, I suspect, continue on when one dies. In this regard, philosophy is an important social practice and further examination of it can guide, at least in part, an assessment of its structure and value as a research method. I agree with Alasdair MacIntyre, who argues that a social practice is

> any coherent and complex form of socially established cooperative human activity through which goods internal to that form of activity are realized in the course of trying to achieve those standards of excellence which are appropriate to, and partially definitive of, that form of activity, with the result that human powers to achieve excellence, and human conceptions of the ends and goods involved, are systematically extended.[3]

This understanding makes clear what does and what does not count as a social practice and it suggests that widely accepted research paradigms are examples of valuable social practices and, therefore, have a specific structure, specific practices, and are done with specific kinds of goals in mind.

MacIntyre goes on to say that any social practice "involves standards of excellence and obedience to rules as well as the achievement of goods."[4] That is, social practices (such as research paradigms) take their cues from an established tradition to create a vision of what is desired for the future. In this idea, MacIntyre provides a framework for discussing whether, and then how, philosophy is structured similarly to other more widely accepted and validated methods of research. Philosophy, as a general social practice, is not dissimilar in basic structure to the practice of gardening—one of my favorite social practices.

As an avid gardener, I have accepted the procedures that have been successful from the gardening tradition and I have accepted the traditional goals of producing good vegetables and developing a closer relationship with the soil. I also adjust and make use of the tradition as it relates to my particular gardening situation, making changes as problems arise and in so doing I improve the traditional practice as it relates to my needs. In the same way, ethnographers, (ethnography being a broadly accepted qualitative research methodology) have a particular set of traditional tools (i.e., observing, journaling, and coding) that are used for understanding particular aspects of lived experience (typically, "culture"), thereby improving its internal practices and systematically extending "the ends and goods involved." Ethnography is a social practice that comfortably fits into the research method category. In the same way, if philosophy's place as a viable method is to be reasonably secured, philosophers must be shown to operate as other researchers do.

To that end, scores of professional philosophers have attempted to explain exactly what philosophers do, what they study, and to what end. This has been particularly true in the last 200 years or so as more and more disciplines have "graduated" out of philosophy (psychology, for example) to operate in their own realms, leaving philosophers, in the opinion of some, with little or nothing to do. As Lewis Feuer said, "not only have we had an end of ideology in America and an end of God in theology, but we have also witnessed evidently an end of philosophy."[5]

In explaining what philosophy is and what philosophers do, scholars such as Feuer are at the same time trying to return philosophy to its origins as a qualitatively relevant enterprise. William Hocking, for example, defined philosophy as operating on two different levels: first, philosophy can be understood simply as "the sum of our beliefs."[6] This could be considered the lay definition of philosophy; most humans, if not all of us, make decisions and take action based on a set of beliefs. However, as a social practice and research methodology, philosophy is much more than this:

"When we speak of philosophy as a science, however, we mean the examination of belief—thinking one's way to a well-grounded set of beliefs. Philosophy holds that we cannot, as human beings, remain satisfied with dumb tenacity in holding our beliefs."[1]

Other philosophers of merit have slightly different descriptions of philosophy's process and purpose. Sidney Hook describes philosophy as having three major aims: helping to understand "the history and nature of our civilization," making "explicit our allegiances to the ideals in behalf of which we are prepared to live, to fight, sometimes even to die," and achieving "awareness and self-consciousness" through the use of logical analysis.[2] Harold Titus writes that, "in a general sense, a person's philosophy is the sum of his fundamental beliefs and convictions." He fleshes out his definition by listing five specific views of philosophy: a personal attitude toward life; a method of reflective thinking; an attempt to gain a view of the whole; logical analysis of language and clarifying of ideas; and a group of specific problems.[3] Giarelli and Chambliss, on the other hand, organize their conception of philosophical research around the goals of clarity (logical accuracy and focus), context (the building up and understanding of the entire qualitative situation under investigation), and consciousness (a grasping of the problem and the need for problem-solving action).[4]

Though these four views contain somewhat different language and have a somewhat different focus, they represent, generally, the essence of philosophic work as a social practice. That essence is, I believe, captured clearly and succinctly in the following "working definition" of philosophic method: "the analysis, clarification, and criticism of the language, concepts, and logic of the ends and means of human experience."[5] This definition characterizes the "what" and the "how" of philosophic method—the conceptual and qualitative nature of philosophy, its social practice characteristics.

The Philosopher's Tools

The first three terms of the above working definition indicate the tools or instruments or the doings of philosophy. That is, philosophers analyze, clarify, and criticize. In analysis, one reduces complex ideas or explicates human situations into understandable, relational concepts. Through analysis, essential concepts that drive practice are extracted from the "boom and buzz" of experience so that they may be more easily debated and understood.

Closely related to analysis is clarification. All too often we simply take for granted or assume that humans have common experiences that lead to commonly held understandings of what we communicate to each other. We are, after all, thrown into the same world with many already established, taken-for-granted ideas of what human experience entails. One responsibility philosophers have is to challenge and ultimately clarify those constructs we use to make sense of the world—constructs often taken for granted rather than clearly and truly understood.

The final tool philosophers traditionally use in their practice is criticism. Criticism entails making judgments as to value. Philosophers judge the instrumental/practical value of those concepts (do they work, and if not, how can we improve them?) for directing practice, and in that critical, interpretive mode build new and better conceptual understandings. The philosopher's tools allow her to investigate and then "mediate" experience and thereby formulate solutions to problems—problems of a specific type. It is also clear that in extracting conceptual constructs that drive actual practice (rather than from some imagined practice), philosophy is qualitative, experiential, and even emotional in its approach to researching lived experience.

The Philosopher's Objects of Inquiry

Just as any type of researcher applies her specific tools to particular types of problems, the philosopher-as-social-practitioner has her own set of objects to which the above tools are applied. The second part of our working definition clearly indicates the philosopher's objects of inquiry. Philosophers apply their traditional tools to the "language" (how we communicate about human experience), the "concepts" (the ideas), and the "logic" (the relationships between the way we think, and communicate) of human experience. In applying the traditional philosophical tools to these essential aspects of lived experience, philosophers provide insights into what, why, and how ideology directs our choices and ensuing actions in lived experience. A philosopher, when doing good work, provides a reasonable understanding of how language, logic, and concepts are playing out in the world and how they might be improved to create a more just and humane society.

Finally, our working definition concludes with the words "means" and "ends" of human experience. That is, philosophers attempt (or should attempt) to make clear the way we think about human experience so that reasonable action (means) might evolve that can lead us to just and good socially established aims (ends) within human experience. We do, after all, hope to make decisions and take action based on sound conceptual understanding. Philosophers investigate real problems that might be alleviated through an improved conceptual understanding, or via creating new conceptual understandings, and point to improved or new connections between those conceptions. It is, in this regard, a social practice that is very qualitative in nature and one that is on par with other, more widely accepted research practices.

The Role of Emotion in Philosophical Work

I suggested above that this working definition might help us to understand the what and the how of philosophical research; however, it does little or nothing to explain the source of that work. That is, it says little about what causes humans to analyze, clarify, and criticize ideas-in-experience in the first place. The pragmatic answer to this question is found in the role emotion plays in human experience. Emotion is the catalyst to thought, and by extension, to learning, including research of all kinds, and particularly so of philosophical endeavors.

On this count, John Dewey argued that emotional disequilibrium or discomfort is the catalyst to reflective thought and is indicative of what he called a "felt difficulty."[6] He also explained how a troubling situation brings with it—in varying degrees, and dependant on one's past experience, natural abilities, and both formal and informal education—a set of suggestions for resolving the problem. These suggestions are, or should be, evaluated for their worth and then applied to the problem at hand with the aim of regaining that lost emotional comfort.[7] Robert R. Sherman puts it this way:

> The fact of the matter is that we do have such feelings. We are surprised or intrigued or revolted or elated by experiences. We like the recommendations that one essayist has, or dislike the proposals put forward by some legislator. Our "guts" are tense, our heads ache, we pace the floor, and our voices rise. These all are indications that we have an "interest" in the matters at hand. Alas, instead of using these as a motive to thought, to elicit the interests, we suppress the feelings; we believe they are in competition with thought and always should be judged the loser.[8]

I think both Dewey and Sherman have it right: emotion, as an indication of a deep and abiding interest, is an essential aspect of a complete act of philosophizing and by implication a complete act of educating; in fact, genuine emotional discomfort is the catalyst without which reflective thought and sound action simply will not, or even cannot, occur. Truly important learning comes from the developed interests derived from lived experience; and though one has to be on guard that the emotion-as-catalyst does not become the sole basis for action, it is essential to understand that emotion is the source of thought. As Sherman said, emotion should not be relegated to "loser" status.

Philosophic Method as a Relevant Mode of Educational Research: The Specifics

The specific relevance philosophical method has for me is in the investigation of educational practice, in this case, CSL. As an associate professor of education, I must be particularly concerned with educational thinking when it comes to understanding philosophic method. To get at its special relevance to education, one need only to replace the phrase "human experience" in our working definition with the more limiting phrase "education" to see exactly what philosophy's role in directing educational practice entails. As the questioners, protectors, and adjusters of educational thinking, philosophers play a very practical role in bringing to light and then addressing basic ideological conflicts. More important, philosophy is essential to educational endeavors, because in education broad social ideological questions appear, are debated, and ultimately passed on or jettisoned. And, I believe that it is in philosophical work that essential educational problems will be initially understood and ultimately solved—a relevantly practical, not aloofly abstract, endeavor.

As to philosophic method's relevance to other forms of research, I believe there exists (or should exist) an especially important and cozy relationship between philosophy and other research—one that is often forgotten or even resisted on the part of philosophers and other researchers alike. Philosophers have the particularly important chore of clarifying our thinking as to conceptual constructs that both clarify experience and direct practice. That methodological purpose is important not simply as a means for philosophers to understand concepts, language, and logic as they operate in real, lived, experience, but it provides a necessary framework that can become the bases for other kinds of research. It's difficult to imagine successful research that is not based on clear philosophical understanding. It's equally difficult to imagine successful philosophizing that isn't, at least sometimes, put to the test by researchers and practitioners using other research methodologies. The two simply must go hand in hand if we are to improve educational practices.

The question of what philosophical method entails is far from dead. One only has to read Richard Rorty's article "Philosophy in America Today" or Kenneth Seeskin's "Never Speculate, Never Explain" to get a feel for the meta-philosophical discussion that began decades ago and continues to this day.[9] In the end, however, I think that philosophy can once again be the vibrant research activity that John Dewey described. Stephen Toulmin, in "The Recovery of Practical Philosophy," traces the history of philosophy relative to the charge of irrelevancy, and in so doing suggests a return to a pre-1630 vision of what philosophical inquiry should be. In the article, Toulmin calls for a philosophy that again takes into account the "oral," the "particular," the "local," and the "timely."[10] This is neither the time nor the place to explicate his entire discussion; it is, however, worth noting that Toulmin's argument is a call to return philosophy to its birthplace as a practical method grounded in the qualitative human experience; I wholeheartedly agree.

In the final analysis, philosophy is a very human enterprise with very real, human consequences. It was from within the human experience that philosophy was born and it is into the human experience that philosophy must always return if it is to remain a vital and relevant social practice. William James described philosophy as "prospective."[11] Indeed it is, for without conceptual clarity we can neither see where we want to go nor how to get there. I think John Dewey best expressed the relevance of philosophy as a practical qualitative research method when he summed up his thoughts in *Reconstruction in Philosophy*:

> When it is acknowledged that under disguise of dealing with ultimate reality, philosophy has been occupied with the precious values embedded in social traditions, that it has sprung from a clash of social ends and from a conflict of inherited institutions with incompatible contemporary tendencies, it will be seen that the task of future philosophy is to

clarify men's ideas as to the social and moral strife of their own day. Its aim is to become so far as is humanly possible an organ for dealing with these conflicts.[12]

My Felt Problem: The Current
Conceptual Muddiness of CSL

As I will explain in the next chapter, the last twenty years or so have seen an explosion of literature related to CSL research and practice, and much of that recent discussion calls for a conceptual/philosophical re-evaluation of CSL—and I certainly agree. The Corporation for National Service and other organizations continue to provide grant monies and technical suggestions for CSL practitioners; however, technical support and money do little to clarify the CSL concept philosophically. This lack of philosophical clarity is particularly problematic for teachers in need of a foundational rationale for CSL practice. One only has to visit the CNS website to see that conceptual muddiness has affected CSL practice. The CNS website defines service learning as "a basis for discovering the common ground among them and to promote discussion about the meaning of service learning."[13] Such definitions might well encourage discussion, but they leave the concept as a whole (as well as each of its individual components) terribly unclear.

According to the National and Community Service Act of 1990, CSL is an educational method

> under which students learn and develop through active participation in thoughtfully organized service experiences that meet actual community needs...; that is integrated into the students' academic curriculum or provides structured time for a student to think, talk, or write about what the student did and saw during the service activity; that provides students with opportunities to use newly acquired skills and knowledge in real-life situations in their own communities; and that enhances what is taught in school by extending student learning beyond the classroom and into the community and helps to foster the development of a sense of caring for others.[14]

Timothy Stanton, a CSL leader and advocate, writes that:

> Service learning appears to be an approach to experiential learning, an expression of values—service to others, which determines the purpose, nature and process of social and educational exchange between learners

(students) and the people they serve, and between experiential education programs and the community organizations with which they work.[15]

Literally dozens of organizations that support CSL explain its conceptual basis differently. One such organization, the Alliance for Service-Learning in Education Reform, defines CSL as:

> a teaching and learning strategy that integrates meaningful community service with instruction and reflection to enrich the learning experience, teach civic responsibility, and strengthen communities.
>
> An exciting, hands-on approach to education, service-learning is taking place in a wide variety of settings: schools, universities, and community-based and faith-based organizations throughout the country. The core concept driving this educational strategy is that by combining service objectives and learning objectives, along with the intent to show measurable change in both the recipient and the provider of the service, the result is a radically-effective transformative method of teaching students.[16]

In *Research Agenda for Combining Service and Learning in the 1990s,* Dwight Giles et al. define CSL as both a program type and a philosophy of education. As a program type,

> Service-learning includes myriad ways that students can perform meaningful service to their communities and to society while engaging in some form of reflection or study that is related to the service. As a philosophy of education, service-learning reflects the belief that education must be linked to social responsibility and that the most effective learning is active and connected to experience in some meaningful way.[17]

Rob Shumer, reporting on a Delphi study of CSL programs, describes the current philosophical problem best when he writes:

> While there is consensus on some aspects of service-learning, for the most part there is still disagreement on the details. There is consensus that service-learning can be envisioned through forms, or types, and that these forms are best understood through specific examples. There is general agreement that service-learning occurs in two general categories: school-based and community-based. Twenty-nine different dichotomous variables ('continua') were named which further describe purposes, goals, processes, and settings of service-learning. All these types and models provide a framework for conceptualizing service-learning in its various configurations; yet none of them are fixed or exact in meaning or description. As powerful and as exciting as any educational innovation and practice, service-learning is still very much an amorphous concept which continues to resist rigid definitions and universal understanding.[18]

Dr. Shumer cautions that CSL should not be penned in by conceptual dogmatism. However, he says CSL remains "amorphous," and as I argue here, confused in its meaning. Until there is philosophical clarity, CSL will continue to ebb and flow with the political/educational tides as it has throughout its history (a history I take up in the next chapter); and sans a clear conceptual understanding, CSL practice in the real world of P–12 education will continue to suffer.

Philosophical Research on CSL

I hope to show you that the story of this book is, in fact, a prototypical example of an emotionally driven search for philosophical answers—answers coming directly out of an experiential quest for emotional comfort, and answers that might prevent others from feeling the same discomfort. It is an attempt to answer the troubling questions of missed potential: why did those PARKnership projects not accomplish more? What did I not know about those grant buzzwords? What constitutes a community? What is service? How can education be "experiential" in CSL? How does human reflection work? Is CSL really a democratic form of education? Can the CSL story be made better? I believe it can; and I believe that bringing some philosophical perspective to its pedagogical structure is the first step in making its story a better one.[19]

The first step in making the CSL story better is to understand whence it came—its conceptual history—and to that I now turn my attention.

CHAPTER THREE

A Brief History of an Educational Idea

Introduction

Tracing an educational reform movement's conceptual evolution is an important endeavor: ignoring the history of an idea can lead to misunderstanding and misguided practice, as layers of contemporary thinking get recklessly piled onto existing theory. In the case of CSL, this kind of reckless piling on has been happening for more than a century now and has caused what I believe is a grand state of conceptual confusion, the sort of confusion that limits practical pedagogical potential. I also believe that discovering how its philosophic muddiness has evolved is a first step toward reclarifying the core ideas of CSL (or any other pedagogy), thereby positively reconstructing its practice. Not only does historic understanding give clues to a pedagogy's philosophic muddiness, it also provides the opportunity to hold on to valuable older ideas, while taking account of contemporary context. On this count, John Dewey suggested that the

> danger in a new movement is that in rejecting the aims and methods of that which it would supplant, it may develop its principles negatively rather than positively and constructively. Then it takes its clew in practice from that which is rejected instead of from the constructive development of its own philosophy.[1]

It is, as Dewey made clear, essential to avoid the mistakes of the past. It is equally important that historically good ideas are not jettisoned along with the bad. To have both requires historical understanding. Albert Adams and Sherrod Reynolds put it this way:

> In examining these ancestral artifacts, some striking similarities to modern practice appear, while once prominent features seem to have been distorted or lost completely. Weaving the tapestry of past and present together is the refrain of openness to experience and change.

Pausing to listen to progressive forefathers engaging in this dialogue
may provide experiential educators with the kind of historical perspective that helps clarify future directions.[2]

Unfortunately, full historical accounts of CSL are relatively
few and far between.[3] However, most scholars of CSL theory trace
its philosophical birth (and I believe, rightly so) to the late-
19th/early-20th-century progressive educational thought that John
Dewey advocated.[4] These CSL historians credit the progressives as
the first to see the necessity of developing an intimate relationship
not only between education and lived experience, but an equally
intimate relationship between schools and democratic communities. Both are essential notions to supporting experiential educational practice. Though the progressives never used the phrase
"Community Service Learning" (or any derivation of it), their
pragmatic philosophy has remained at the core of CSL theory and
practice and they should well be seen as CSL's conceptual founders.

Other CSL advocates, however, trace the movement back only
as far as the 1960s and 1970s when the actual phrase "service-
learning" was first used.[5] The "pioneer" rebirth of progressive
theory in the 1960s and '70s included the 1967 coining of the
phrase service-learning, which in turn lead to major growth of the
CSL pedagogy in both private and public schools throughout the
1970s.[6] My concern here is not to laud credit upon any particular
historic group; rather, it is to glean the important clarifying notions from both movements, the progressives and the pioneers (or
anyone else, for that matter), to help clear the conceptual fog of
present CSL theory and practice.

Community Service, Education and American Character

Americans have a relatively long history of individual and
communal voluntary public service as part of our national character. This history certainly predates the pragmatic philosophy initially developed by William James and C.S Peirce. In fact, Alexis
de Tocqueville, the famed French cultural commentator, argued in
1835 that our republican political framework combined with our
lack of aristocratic hierarchy *demanded* that individuals serve society voluntarily; if not, Tocqueville suggested, selfish individualism would destroy our democratic experiment.[7] The American
notion of democratic service can be found in familiar tales of barn

raisings, church construction, and caring for families fallen ill, as well as in political participation. As Robert Bellah and his colleagues note in *Habits of the Heart*, the tension between our very American sense of individualism and our equally strong sense of commitment to community continues to play out in policy-making, educational and otherwise, today as it has throughout our history.[8] This tension is derived from our exceptional beliefs in the ideology of democracy, the power of education, and the responsibility of the individual; and it is vital to the understanding of CSL (and one I take up more completely in a later chapter).[9]

While communities busied themselves building the young nation, education came to be seen as necessary to maintaining democratic life and democratic institutions. Horace Mann saw that "enlightened" participation must be encouraged and civic skills taught in public schools so that American democracy could survive.[10] Public education, particularly, blossomed as a result of Horace Mann's (and others) thinking about education and the development of democracy. Not until the late-19th century, however, did these three essential democratic notions (individualism, commitment to community, and education) come together in CSL-like educational practice.

Penn Normal School: An Early Example of CSL in Practice

The Civil War not only forcefully reunited the southern and the northern states, but also brought together community, service, and education for the first time in U.S. history. Out of the fiery battles of the Civil War came a newly emancipated slave population that had to be educated. To thrive economically and to participate as American citizens, ex-slaves needed democratic education.[11] Following the Civil War, African American educational institutions such as Tuskegee and Hampton provided those necessary educational services in the American South, particularly through ex-slave education.[12] Penn Normal School (PNS) in South Carolina approached the problem of educating these new citizens by combining community service with public education: it was one of the earliest experiments with CSL education.

Rosa B. Cooley and Grace Bigelow House established Penn Normal, Agricultural and Industrial School in St. Helena, South Carolina, in 1862. The school's mission was to educate ex-slaves so that they could deal successfully with their newly won freedom.

Though Cooley and House never used any of the contemporary language of CSL when describing the activities at PNS, it's clear that community, service, and learning were intimately linked in the school's educational practice. In his foreword to *School Acres: An Adventure in Rural Education,* Paul Kellogg noted that Cooley and House found:

> The experience of Penn in education "of the people, by the people, for the people" not only plays luminously on the needs of rural districts the country over, but upon a dilemma confronting our cities. Miss Cooley reveals how the New England school of the "three R's" with its academic ramifications fell short when it came to training-for-life under the changing conditions of the rural South. She sets forth the strategy and spirit of the two revolutions at Penn School—how the life of the farms was brought into the classrooms, and then how through the school acres and other extramural activities the process was reversed and the educational impulse was spread to the ends of the island.[13]

PNS clearly operated on a conceptual foundation similar to that which progressive educational philosophers would come to emphasize: "to learn it is to live it."[14]

The PNS philosophy that as essential democratic institutions, schools should be conceptualized as inexorably tied to the broader community was another indication that Cooley and House practiced an early version of the CSL pedagogy. Students, citizens, and teachers approached "felt" community problems together through projects that blurred the classroom/community line. The school became a vital part of the community rather than a separate institution:

> The children return to their homes each evening and connect those homes with the school with an unbroken intimacy. The mass of children in a thousand communities in the South cannot go to boarding schools. The rural teacher must be interested in the family as well as in the child and the larger community interests are as important as the classrooms.[15]

The PNS philosophy also held that for a school to be an essential part of the community, it must be "elastic" and start with problem-driven interests of students and their families.[16] Student-centered educational practice, an intimate interaction between school and community, and experiential learning were all harbingers of progressive educational theory generally, and CSL particularly.

Pragmatist Support for CSL

The pedagogy put into practice at such places as PNS was put into formal philosophical theory just as PNS expanded its practice. Progressive educators and philosophers of the newly created pragmatic school of philosophy theorized that schools in a democracy must be tools of the community and extensions of the home. Notions of community, education, and service intertwined as a result of changes in educational philosophy that was driven by a shift in the notion of philosophy generally and epistemology particularly. In advancing William James' pragmatism, John Dewey, William H. Kilpatrick, and Paul Hanna (among others) talked of an educational philosophy that had as its starting point the primacy of student experience.[17] The change in educational thinking mirrored the shift in general philosophical inquiry away from abstraction and to lived experience.

John Dewey argued on this point that "the business of schooling tends to become a routine empirical affair unless its aims and methods are animated by such a broad and sympathetic survey of its place in contemporary life."[18] That is, if schools are to succeed as vital democratic institutions, they must be directly involved in the life of their communities. Pragmatic philosophers held that good education, like useful philosophy, must approach its aims by beginning with authentically felt problems. Absent this, both practices (philosophy and education) degenerate to mere abstraction. Feeling and facing real community problems—rather than artificially created ones— fosters reflective, critical inquiry and also encourages young citizens to actively participate in transforming their community.

William James' Call to National Service

Numerous educational scholars, writing about the emergence of national service generally and CSL specifically, correctly credit William James with suggesting a transformation of military pride into peaceful, civically organized communal activity similar to CSL.[19] In his speech "The Moral Equivalent of War," James proposed the following:

> If now—and this is my idea—there were, instead of military conscription, a conscription of the whole youthful population to form for a certain number of years a part of the army enlisted against Nature, the injustice

would tend to be evened out, and numerous other goods to the common-wealth would remain blind as the luxurious classes now are blind, to man's relations to the globe he lives on, and to the permanently sour and hard foundations of his higher life.[20]

William James' community service ideas and pragmatic philosophy were the catalysts for progressive educational change. This change in philosophy generally and philosophy of education specifically began the conceptual evolution that became the CSL educational philosophy.

John Dewey's Democratic Education

John Dewey did not call it CSL, but what he advocated was similar in both aim and method to what the Penn Normal School initiated near the end of the Civil War and what contemporary CSL educators claim to do today. In 1899, Dewey delivered a series of lectures specifically for teachers. These talks contained the beginnings of a philosophy of education on which CSL practice might be based. Dewey described the kinds of approaches to education that fit the democratic experience, debunked traditional learning theory, and prescribed similar practices to those found at the Penn Normal School.

Echoing the educational practice found at schools such as Penn Normal School, Dewey conceived schools as extensions of the family and important community institutions. Dewey said about this relationship:

> If we take an example from an ideal home, where the parent is intelligent enough to recognize what is best for the child, and is able to supply what is needed, we find the child learning through the social converse and constitution of the family. There are certain points of interest and value to him in the conversation carried on: statements are made, inquiries arise, topics are discussed, and the child continually learns. He states his experiences. His misconceptions are corrected.... Now, if we organize and generalize all of this, we have the ideal school. There is no mystery about it, no wonderful discovery of pedagogy or educational theory. It is simply a question of doing systematically and in a large, intelligent, and competent way what for various reasons can be done in most households only in a comparatively meager and haphazard manner.[21]

Clearly Dewey was talking about a notion of schooling that Cooley and House in South Carolina had already embraced in practice: a democratic institution intimately connected to and driven by community problems and citizen needs.

William H. Kilpatrick's Project Method

William H. Kilpatrick, a student of Dewey and a follower of pragmatism, developed educational concepts that advanced progressive educational thinking, and by extension, contemporary CSL practice. In his 1922 essay, "The Project Method," Kilpatrick discussed public education and its role in a democratic community and explained his own ideas of "purposeful acts" related to learning. Based on Dewey's philosophy of democratic education, Kilpatrick argued that the project method of teaching was essential to extending democratic community:

> As the purposeful act is thus the typical unit of the worthy life in a democratic society, so also should it be made the typical unit of school procedure. We of America have for years increasingly desired that education be considered as life itself and not as a mere preparation for later living. If we apply this criterion to the common run of American schools we find exactly the discouraging results indicated above. It is the thesis of this paper that these evil results must inevitably follow the effort to found our educational procedure on an unending round of set tasks in conscious disregard of the element of dominant purpose in those who perform the tasks.[22]

Kilpatrick's contributions to CSL theory are various and immense. I believe his most important and enduring contribution, however, is not his explication of the purposeful act or the project method's relationship to democracy. Other progressive educators, i.e., Dewey, had made those points already. Rather, Kilpatrick is important to CSL's philosophy because of the specificity of his suggestions for educational practice. The steps of the "project method" contained most of the components that contemporary CSL educators suggest. He wrote:

> the following steps have been suggested: purposing, planning, executing, and judging. It is in accord with the general theory here advocated that the child as far as possible take each step himself. The function of the purpose and the place of thinking in the process need but be mentioned. Attention may be called to the fourth step, that the child as he grows older may increasingly judge the result in terms of the aim and with increasing care and success draw from the process its lessons for the future.[23]

These "steps" were obvious antecedents to contemporary CSL practice and echoed John Dewey's description of the thinking process.[24]

Paul Hanna and the Progressive Education Association

The pragmatic/progressive movement in public education strengthened throughout the decade of the 1920s as Dewey and Kilpatrick argued for progressive educational reform. In 1931, Dewey repeated the call for Kilpatrick's project method approach, advocating it as a "way out of educational confusion," and George Counts took the progressives to task while maintaining the hope that community-based schools could "build a new social order."[25] In 1936, a study was published by the Progressive Education Association that looked specifically at community service activities by a variety of youth organizations around the country. Until the 1970s, the PEA study was the most ambitious of its kind, looking at community service among youth. Its theoretical clarity is especially impressive.

The 1936 PEA study took the form of a survey directed by Paul Hanna. The survey team sent questionnaires to youth organizations asking for descriptions of community service projects and specific benefits for both server and served. The study was undertaken during the Depression and at the height of social programs such as the Civilian Conservation Corps and other "alphabet" Depression remedies.[26] The survey responses provided engaging stories of youth solving community problems through service projects; however, the more impressive aspect of the study for the present discussion was the clear theory that accompanied the survey results. It was the pen of William H. Kilpatrick that provided the philosophical basis for the study. Following an initial discussion couching educational practice within democracy, Kilpatrick argued that there are specific notions that must be part of any democratic community educational philosophy (my apologies for the length of the following quotes):

> As for the problem before us now, we wish to build up in our young people a sensitiveness to such community deficiencies as they can help to correct. We wish them to be so sensitive to possible community improvements that they will of themselves see new opportunities and wish to take hold of them. To sense such a situation so as to be stirred by it to action—this is the first step in dealing with that situation. The second

step follows at once. If we are really stirred to action and wish to act intelligently, we shall study the situation to see what should be done. This neglected spot in our village is (by step 1) an eyesore, to be improved if possible. Now (step 2) we ask what can be done about it, or what we should do. Shall we ask the owner to clean it up? Or shall we ask his permission to make a playground of it? What would it cost to make a playground? What kind of clearing and grading would be necessary? It is at any rate quite clear that good study would be necessary to answer these questions and decide what to do. The third step, of how to do it, follows so closely upon the second as often to merge into it. We could not decide what to do until we decided, at least within limits, how to do it. So here we have the further detailed study necessary for making all the plans. The fourth step is the execution of the plan. Here we have the kind of study that goes with carrying out the plan, and particularly the study that goes with watching how well our plans work out. We shall probably have to revise our plans as we try them out. If so, more study and learning. The fifth step is the backward view: Now that we have finished, what have we learned? How could we do it better another time? What lessons of any or all kinds shall we draw?[27]

Kilpatrick's discussion contained the theoretical essentials of CSL. He fleshed out these important notions in finishing the introduction to the PEA study:

> Why, next, do we wish community activities? The answer follows hard upon the preceding. A community activity can have a reality and a challenge that no lesser activity can properly have. Moreover, it serves to bring the youthful group (school or church or club, etc.) into desirable intimate contact with the surrounding community. To do something which others count significant ranks very high among the satisfying and steadying influences in life. For the young to feel that their activities have community significance is to accord to them a worth and standing that will call out the best the young have to give. Why "cooperative community activities?" What, finally, is meant by cooperative community activities, and why are they desired? Here again we build on the preceding. By cooperative community activities we mean those in which many share, preferably the old along with the young.[28]

Paul Hanna further developed the community education concept set out by Kilpatrick in describing his research criteria for good community educational practice. He explained that if community service was to be a vital pedagogical approach, then the participating students must

> 1. Sense its social significance. 2. Have a part in planning the project. In a democracy, probably no learnings are more significant than those

which result from social experiences in which a group need is faced cooperatively, analyzed, possible solutions projected, tentative plans agreed upon, and the task eventually culminated. 3. Have some sporting chance of carrying the project proposed through to more or less successful conclusion. 4. Accept the responsibility for success or failure of a project. Any vital learning experience is incomplete until the plan and its execution have been evaluated in terms of successes and/or failures in the social environment. 5. Actually grow in total personality as a result of the work undertaken.[29]

Importantly, particularly in light of contemporary CSL practice (and discussed in the ensuing chapters), Hanna provided three essential evaluative criterions for a project's impact on a community:

1. Any project must culminate in the actual improvement of living in the community. 2. Projects must clearly be an obligation of youth as well as adulthood. 3. In so far as possible, *projects must get at the basic problems of improving social welfare* (emphasis mine).[30]

Finally, Hanna directed his readers back to John Dewey in echoing the notion that education mirror the way humans think and act to solve "felt" problems. Hanna remarked:

This thinking process has the following distinguishing phases: (a) Something is at stake. A state of confusion or disequilibrium has occurred. We are aroused to take action to achieve a better adjustment. (b) The difficulty is located and defined. No intelligent effort at improvement can be made until the nature and source of the unsatisfactory aspects of the situation are clarified. (c) An hypothesis is developed for meeting the difficulty and improving the conditions. This projection of proposals and plans is the most important technique which man possesses for continued progress. (d) A detailed plan of operation with continued reflective criticism of each step of the plan is worked out. (e) The best experimental method in terms of the purpose, materials and tools available, and the unpredictable elements which arise in the process of carrying out the plan must be utilized. (f) When the plan has been carried out the results must be measured in terms of the values anticipated at the beginning, and the plan itself must be criticized for possible improvement. Furthermore, the enterprise must be judged in terms of its effect on those who participated in its solution; that is, it must be judged in terms of its enrichment of personalities.[31]

Clearly this conceptual history of CSL as developing from progressive educational philosophy, and briefly outlined here, suggests numerous sources and possible solutions to my own PARKnership "confusion."

Progressivism Wanes

The late 1930s brought Nazi Germany to the fore of international concern. Adolf Hitler's military movements distracted America from educational concerns and turned all thought to its inevitable involvement in WWII. Throughout the Depression years of the 1920s and 1930s (and to some degree as a response to the Depression), many schools practiced the progressive CSL pedagogy; but by 1940, progressivism in educational practice waned. Though progressive thought remained a small part of school operations in some districts, the progressive/CSL concept generally lost favor with politicians, the American public, and educational critics who viewed it as "soft pedagogy." President Dwight Eisenhower went so far as to lay many national problems, educationally and otherwise, at the feet of John Dewey himself. [32]

By the early 1950s, Kilpatrick and a few of his ardent followers represented what was left of the progressive educational movement. They carried the CSL concept forward through their work with the Citizenship Education Project at Columbia University's Teachers College. With generous support from the Carnegie Foundation and other benefactors, CEP continued to use Kilpatrick's ideas particularly in "citizenship education."

However, by the mid 1950s, little was left of the progressive movement: the PEA changed its name and then disbanded in 1955; the 1957 launch of Sputnik pushed progressive educational philosophy and practice into a stasis; and politicians called on schools to institute more traditionally oriented academic instruction rather than the supposed soft pedagogy of progressive/CSL epistemology—Congress going so far as to fund this shift through the National Defense Education Act.[33]

Though the conceptual history of CSL and the progressive movement in education are not precisely the same, the fading of progressive philosophy from the forefront of the American public-school debate took with it the conceptual notion of CSL. It would be nearly fifteen years before CSL regained its foothold in educational thought and practice. The rebirth of the CSL concept came about in one of its original birthplaces—the American South. This rebirth came not in P–12 education, but in the endeavors of southern universities.

The Rebirth of the CSL Concept: The "Pioneers"

In 1967, out of such programs as Peace Corps, Volunteers in Service to America (VISTA), and Donald Eberly's National Service suggestions, came the first use of the phrase "service-learning." [34] The Southern Regional Education Board established a service-learning internship program in 1964. By 1967, SREB's program involved more than 300 college students. William O'Connell explained in 1972,

> The term service-learning has been adopted as best describing this combination of the performance of a useful service for society and the disciplined interpretation of that experience for an increase in knowledge and in understanding one's self. The coupling of action and reflection has implications for both education and vocation and also is seen as more than a useful technique for performing a task or for educational enrichment. It leads to practice in the development of a lifestyle.[35]

The SREB CSL program did not develop from a detailed philosophical discussion, as provided by scholars such as Paul Hanna 35 years earlier. However, SREB did reintroduce some of the educational practices that had gone missing during the 1950s. The specific concept of CSL, and experiential education generally, found its way back into educational reform talk and practice throughout the American South at least partially because the SREB internship program grew so successfully.

With the Vietnam War continuing and thousands of young Americans hoping for possible service alternatives to the draft, the political, social, and educational will were available for a resurgence of CSL-like practice and theory. [36] In 1969, the Atlanta Service-Learning Conference began "with 500 students engaged in service-learning projects."[37] The Atlanta project culminated in a conference and publication of "Atlanta Service-learning Conference Report—1970." In 1971, ACTION, a federal agency, was established to bring together and oversee such programs as Peace Corps, VISTA, Retired Senior Volunteer Program (RSVP), Service Corps of Retired Executives (SCORE), and the National Student Volunteer Program (NSVP). Also in 1971, the National Society for

Experiential Education (NSEE) was brought into being and advocated for CSL education.

In 1972, ACTION published *High School Student Volunteers.* This manual provided a discussion of volunteer programs in high schools and suggested how such programs might be established and run. The authors listed three "essential ingredients" for a successful high school volunteer program, somewhat reminiscent of Paul Hanna's suggestions from the 1930s:

> 1. The community must have needs that can be met by student volunteers. 2. Students must be interested in working hard on a volunteer basis to meet those needs. 3. The school must support the effort by coordinating individual projects into a coherent program.[38]

The authors of the manual also argued that only schools could focus and reinforce the volunteers' experiences to ensure that real learning resulted. They were convinced that "reviewing their community work in class, students become better volunteers; drawing on their experience in the field, volunteers become better students."[39] The ACTION authors explained why service and learning were important for students and how the two might be incorporated into P–12 education as a communal endeavor. The publication of the ACTION manual was particularly important for CSL's rebirth, because except for a few "fringe schools,"[40] CSL had not been part of educational practice for the 35 years prior to its publication.

Through federal agencies such as ACTION and professional organizations such as the Association for Experiential Education, CSL grew both as a concept and a practice, particularly on college campuses during the middle and late 1970s. For the most part, however, CSL remained on the periphery of educational reform as a somewhat underdeveloped internship idea. In 1979, the National Student Volunteer Program was renamed and became the National Center for Service Learning (NCSL) and published the first issue of the journal *Synergist*, in which are found the "Three Principles of Service-Learning." These principles became the basis of a widening philosophical discussion returning to the question of how to conceptualize CSL.[41]

The rebirth of CSL-like educational practices, manifested in the establishment of the NCSL, ran aground as many educational initiatives have in the past, and in much the same way. In 1980, the election of Ronald Reagan ushered in a conservative backlash to progressive educational policy, going so far as to suggest the abolishment of the U.S. Department of Education. This backlash once again brought a temporary end to the progressive/pioneering education reforms sourced in the late-19th/early-20th centuries and reborn in the 1970s. What Sputnik had done in the late 1950s, conservative educational policy did in the 1980s. The NCSL was shut down in 1982, and CSL once again disappeared from educational talk and practice for most of the decade. It was, however, a relatively brief silence for CSL theory and practice.

In 1985, several college and university presidents formed Campus Compact, giving voice once again to the idea that college and university students should learn through serving their communities. In 1986, the federal government established Youth Service America, which advocated and supported student service by providing both funding and training. However, it was not until 1989 that CSL had its third rebirth as an educational reform for P–12 education in the United States.

In 1989, the Johnson Foundation sponsored the Wingspread Conference on Youth Service at which more than 70 organizations collaborated to write "ten principles of good service-learning practice." The Wingspread report was the first conceptual reformulation of CSL since the late-1960s and early-1970s internship programs and the first of many conceptual descriptions of CSL developed in the 1990s. I believe the Wingspread principles are the most complete attempt to clarify CSL conceptually since the early part of the 20th century and these ten principles remain a widely accepted guide for present CSL practice.

Though the concepts contained in the Wingspread document are less than complete, they capture the general character of CSL. Following a brief "preamble," the conference participants suggested that a successful CSL program:

1. Engages people in responsible and challenging actions for the common good. 2. Provides structured opportunities for people to reflect critically on their service experience. 3. Articulates clear service and learning goals for everyone involved. 4. Allows for those with needs to define those needs. 5. Clarifies the responsibilities of each person and organization involved. 6. Matches service providers and service needs through a process that recognizes changing circumstances. 7. Expects genuine, active, and sustained organizational commitment. 8. Includes training, supervision monitoring, support, recognition, and evaluation to meet

service and learning goals. 9. Insures that the time commitment for service and learning is flexible, appropriate, and in the best interests of all involved. 10. Is committed to program participation by and with diverse populations.[42]

These principles became the rules of practice for CSL, and though they did not answer the numerous philosophical questions asked by progressive educators (and taken up in the ensuing chapters of this book), they did provide some guidance and a framework from which contemporary CSL advocates could start.

In 1990, to encourage the civic engagement called for by the Wingspread principles, Congress passed, and President George H. Bush Sr. signed, the National and Community Service Act of 1990. This first in a series of federally supported grant programs made $75 million available through the Points of Light Foundation and the Commission on National and Community Service to support community service activities.

CSL partnerships between communities and schools (both public and private) were encouraged through the awarding of grant money. In 1993, as a centerpiece of his first term in office, President Bill Clinton gave further life to the CSL movement by signing the National and Community Trust Act. This legislation created the Corporation for National Service, a federal agency that would administer both AmeriCorps and Learn and Serve America programs.[43] Learn and Serve America, several professional organizations, and a handful of major universities pushed to institute CSL education.[44] As advocates, these organizations still provide the means and much of the research support for CSL in schools at every level that was initiated three decades ago.

Contemporary CSL Theory and Practice

Since the creation of CNS and partly because of it, there has been a rather impressive growth in scholarship surrounding CSL focused on both its theory and practice—so impressive in number as to make it impossible to cover completely here (a recent search for scholarship on "service learning" on JSTOR returned no fewer than 12,000 matches). Much of that scholarship is reminiscent of its progressive pragmatic history, but certainly important in its consideration of contemporary social and educational contexts. Given this contemporary orientation, I would be remiss in not mentioning several current themes common to the literature as well as some of the more influential scholars working within those themes—those who have ushered CSL along and into the 21st century and who provide some of the groundwork for what I conceptualize later as strong and weak understandings of CSL theory and practice.

CSL and Content

The first two themes common to more recent scholarship on CSL are focused on content learning—what I call "aims" in the next chapter and what others have called "outcomes." The first of these thematic orientations is directed toward practical suggestions for restructuring typical course work, mostly at the university level, to imbed a CSL project model. The most important and best known of these efforts is found in a series produced by the American Association for Higher Education.[45] That series, AAHE's *Series on Service-Learning in the Disciplines* (published from 1997 through 2002), is quite expansive in its range of content.

The AAHE Series includes collections on economics, religious studies, Christian ethics, women's studies, biology, management, philosophy, history, medicine, psychology— to list a few—and from important thinkers in the field. This series, in addition to numerous individual journal pieces, provide some very helpful guidance for incorporating CSL into content, and though most are oriented toward higher education, certainly lessons can be gleaned for P–12 teachers as well. As pieces that focus mostly on content, these are typically suggestions for "weaker" versions of CSL, focused on subject matter learning rather than broader issues of democratic character and institutional change.

CSL and Research Methodology

A second arena of interest of late is done with the purpose of defending CSL as a viable educational endeavor—quality research that shows CSL is equal to or better than traditional modes of "delivering" content. I expect as time goes along, these endeavors will grow even more quickly as resources become tighter and the public demands evidence of educational success at every level. The general suggestion for research on CSL is that a broad array of approaches must be used, both quantitative and qualitative, to investigate its impact on expected outcomes. I provide a list of such research and suggestions for future research in an appendix to this book. I will mention a few collections specifically here to which the reader might turn to learn of the various research emphases current in the field. The first of these is a series published by Information Age Publishing and, importantly for my purposes, has a strong P–12 focus. That series, entitled *Advances in Service-Learning Research*, includes *Deconstructing Service-Learning: Research Exploring Context, Participation, and Impacts, Improving Service-Learning Practice: Research on Models to Enhance Impacts, and Advancing Knowledge in Service-Learning: Research to Transform the Field*, among several others.[46]

A second resource for help in conducting research on CSL is *The Measure of Service Learning: Research Scales to Assess Student Experiences* by Robert Bringle, Mindy Phillips, and Michael Hudson.[47] The authors provide scales developed to measure a variety of different learning outcomes, including content learning, attitudes, critical thinking, and even moral development. Finally, there is one journal specifically created for CSL scholarship. That journal, the *Michigan Journal of Community Service Learning*, edited by Jeffrey Howard, regularly publishes research-oriented pieces, including a special issue on the direction CSL research might take.[48] Work on research models and reporting the results of actual research is vital to growing CSL at every level and can be the means for measuring relative weakness or strength of CSL projects.

CSL and Democratic Citizenship

In response to the clear weakening of "public life and civic judgment" among contemporary generations of Americans,[49] numerous scholars point to CSL's potential to reinvigorate democratic participation. This area of CSL scholarship flourished in the late 1980s and early 1990s, particularly at colleges and universities. It proposes that when done well, CSL can help develop what Bellah and his colleagues call democratic "habits of the heart."[50] Timothy Stanton writes in this regard, "'service learning' is a key to ensuring the development of graduates who will participate in society actively, ethically, and with an informed critical habit of mind;"[51] I certainly agree, and there is ample evidence that such democratic participation has atrophied, particularly of late.

The notion that CSL can accomplish such a democratic reinvigoration is reflective of what I will later describe as the weaker version of CSL, and as that reinvigoration becomes more institutionally critical, I suggest CSL becomes "stronger." In terms of this democratically weaker version of CSL, much research and conceptual work continues. Conceptually speaking, scholars such as Benjamin Barber, Richard Battistoni, Joel Westheimer, and Joseph Kahne, among numerous others continue to probe the value that well-structured CSL programs can provide for developing the traits needed for a vibrant democracy.

More specifically, Battistoni has suggested that a well-conceived CSL program can incorporate a "civic view" of service, one based on the understanding that "free democratic communities depend on mutual responsibility and that rights without obligations are ultimately not sustainable."[52] Barber approaches CSL from what he calls "strong democracy," one in which civic engagement is "persuasively progressive and democratic."[53] Westheimer and Kahne outline three versions of citizenship that CSL might engender: the "personally responsible," the "participatory," and the "justice oriented"—each of the three reflecting increasingly "stronger" conceptions of CSL.[54] Not surprisingly, these and most CSL theorists credit John Dewey with first articulating the important connection between democracy and democratic schooling.

CSL and Social Justice/Diversity

A more recent concern among CSL scholars is that of social justice with particular emphasis on diversity, and which is, at least in part, reflective of the critical theory perspective that I will explain briefly below. The social-justice orientation of such scholars is also indicative of the move from a weaker to a stronger understanding of the CSL pedagogy. Unfortunately, the work of social-justice scholars is directed almost entirely toward higher education. The most important collection that places CSL within a social-justice orientation is *Race, Poverty, and Social Justice*, edited by José Z. Calderón and published in 2007. Though I take up social justice in CSL more completely in the chapter on strong CSL, I will take a moment here to briefly describe the issues that contemporary CSL scholars suggest a social-justice-oriented CSL program might endeavor to address.

In the introduction to *Race, Poverty, and Social Justice*, Calderón writes "our purpose...is to provide examples of how service learning can be integrated into courses addressing social justice issues. At the same time, it is about demonstrating the power of service learning in advancing a course content that is community based and socially engaged."[55] In fact, this collection takes up very typical social-justice issues including race, the plight of day laborers, homelessness, and so on.

On the other hand, the courses, projects, and theory described in this collection (and indicative of most social-justice-oriented CSL projects) fall short of the strong version I advocate for here for one simple reason: the majority of such projects are oriented toward student "appreciation" of the problem (the internal) and rarely include true social action toward changing institutional policy (the external). This shortcoming is demonstrated most ironically in a CSL public-policy course where students learned that "through social justice advocacy, public policy can be improved and political and social institutions changed for the better," though the students themselves did not attempt to institute change.[56] Certainly, one must understand that public policy impacts marginalized groups in profound ways before one can become an agent of change—such CSL courses should be commended for that. However, at its strongest, I believe CSL can provide the opportunity to actually act for such change at every educational level.

The Critical Turn

Current CSL theory has turned much attention to what is generally called "critical theory" and educational practice based on that theory, "critical pedagogy." Critical theory as a tradition has taken hold quite powerfully in educational scholarship, including CSL, and has a rather sturdy history. Coming historically from the insightful work of such folks as Paulo Freire, Jürgen Habermas, Herbert Marcuse, Walter Benjamin and the more contemporary work of Peter McLaren, Henry Giroux, and bell hooks (among numerous others, including importantly, feminist theorists), critical theorists rely particularly on the thinking of Karl Marx, Sigmund Freud, and Max Weber (among others) to critique economic and social constructs of oppression, individual constructions of self, and how the interaction of the two impact broad understandings of human experience. Current CSL scholarship has made use of critical theory to advance it as a form of critical pedagogy, particularly in higher education.

In an article tracing this critical turn in contemporary CSL scholarship, Tania Mitchell argues (and I think she is correct) that when "unpacked" the literature suggests "it is difficult to create a definition that elicits consensus amongst practitioners":

> A growing segment of the service-learning literature in higher education assumes that community service linked to learning is inherently connected to concerns of social justice.... At the same time, there is an emerging body of literature arguing that the traditional service-learning approach is not enough.... This literature advocates a "critical" approach to community service learning with an explicit aim toward social justice.[57]

Mitchell then goes about perusing the literature, noting that this critical turn began as early as 1997 in the work of Robert Rhoads and was increasingly given life by such scholars as Marullo, Wade, and Boyle-Baise, among others. Finally, Mitchell suggests distinctions that mark a difference between "traditional service-learning" and "critical service-learning."

I have to admit having a love-hate relationship with critical theorists and critical pedagogues. The love comes particularly with some of the insights that early critical theorists have provided into contemporary living ("postmodern living," if you will). I think it's reflective of a generally healthy philosophical skepticism and mode of experiencing the world, one that philosophers have adopted since at least the time of Socrates. The hate, on the other hand, comes with two contentions asserted earlier: sans an initial grounding in actual practice, contemporary theory quite easily gets "recklessly" piled onto existing conceptions; and secondly, philosophy can and should speak plainly if its implications for practice are to be clearly understood. I believe that critical theory is particularly guilty of recklessly piling on via its somewhat mysterious language.

Both of these tendencies leave practitioners, particularly those outside of higher education, scratching their heads, wondering what it all means for actual practice. Again, peruse the literature: much of the "out-of-touch" scholarship I alluded to in Chapter Two comes from critical theory. In the end, however, I agree with Mitchell on all counts: CSL, when understood from its roots, is inherently "critical"—it grows from the very critical tradition of pragmatism. I also agree with Mitchell that critical theorists can help the CSL story, but only if its basic constructs are first examined for the insights they provide for actual practice.

Historical Implications for Practice: Looking Back to the Future

In an interesting and insightful article predicting yet another demise of CSL education, Don Hill "looked back" to the year 2010 and tried to analyze what went wrong. He gives ten reasons for CSL's complete disappearance from the educational scene. Though each reason he gives has a sense of its own, it is his second reason that explains my present felt problem with CSL education—and that is the subject of the rest of this study. Hill looked back and predicted that service-learning would remain

> an ambiguous or fuzzy concept to the majority of teachers. In order to meet political pressures to allocate government and foundation money to a wide variety of eager schools, the definition of service learning was commonly broadened to the point where almost anything could fit. Service learning, by becoming everything, became almost nothing.[58]

The history of CSL surely involves numerous other players not mentioned here. But the point of this necessarily brief historical outline is that the incredible growth of CSL in practice has not had a corresponding growth in conceptual understanding. In fact, CSL has taken on a confusing, amorphous character as groundless practice races beyond sound foundational understanding. In light of the pendulum-like wavering of CSL history, I believe it must be first soundly grounded in a strong conceptual foundation out of which good practice can be built. For CSL to survive the ever-shifting sands of educational criticism, the driving philosophical concepts of reasonable aims, community, service, experiential learning, and reflection, must be clearly understood in the context of CSL education. I find Don Hill's prediction quite prophetic—and here we are, at the beginning of 2011. I believe it's time to prevent CSL from becoming "everything" so that it might remain a very important something to individual, communal, and educational reconstruction, reform, and practice.

CHAPTER FOUR

Aims

Introduction

In my initial sales pitch for valuing philosophy as a viable educational research endeavor, I argued that such research entailed an analysis of the goals (the ends) of educational endeavors as well as the methods (the means) utilized to meet those goals. In the chapters that follow, I will discuss the particular concepts (community, service, experiential epistemology, and reflection) that drive CSL as a pedagogical approach. In this chapter, I lay out what I believe are the reasonable destinations toward which CSL projects can lead, when well conceived. As I often tell my students, you can't plan a trip until you know where you're going.

Establishing and clarifying educational aims is without question an essential, philosophically practical task. Richard Millard Jr. and Peter Bertocci go so far as to suggest:

> Every educational system or body of educational practices does involve some set of ends or aims felt to be of sufficient importance or value to be perpetuated, or strengthened, or created in individuals and the community by the particular education as such. Without these, no education would, in fact, occur.[1]

I certainly agree, as long as those goals are conceived of and constructed from within the particular educational context, rather than from without that context, as is increasingly the case in the contemporary No Child Left Behind (NCLB) world of educational policy and practice. More on that point momentarily.

In addition to the important road-map quality that sound educational aims have, there is the historically difficult fact that such goals are extremely contentious, often pitting varying special-interest groups, parents, educators, and individual community members against one another with our nation's legal system often becoming the final battleground for such debates. And it makes sense: education is the means by which those values we hold dear are passed on to future generations, and education is the means by which outdated or outgrown beliefs are discarded and replaced with new ones.[2] As Susanne Langer explained, determining educational aims

> cannot but draw in vast further questions of the aims of human societies, the ultimate values that set up these aims, our basic ideals of society and individual life. Perused seriously it may lead to entirely new definitions of "society," "life," "individual," "purpose," "action," and other terms.[3]

And, as Henry Perkins has made clear, American public education has historically been called upon regularly to solve any and all perceived social problems.[4] To avoid a spiraling discussion that would require an additional volume, I will stick with aims directly entailed in CSL practice and avoid taking sides on the public school's role as panacea-to-solving-social-ills, as well as larger philosophical discussions such as those suggested by Langer.

From where or from whom should educational aims come? I believe it is essential that aims are not "assigned" from outside the particular educational context—CSL or otherwise. Sound goals, of any educational approach, are only sound if they are entailed in practice rather than imposed from outside the practice. Aims, correctly understood, are just as much a part of the experienced educational situation as are the means utilized to meet those aims. When aims are determined from outside of actual context, they are artificial goals that limit, rather than open, possibilities for practice. As John Dewey cautioned, externally established educational aims are problematic because they

> assume ends lying outside our activities; ends foreign to the concrete makeup of the situation; ends which issue from some outside source. Then the problem is to bring our activities to bear upon the realization of these externally supplied ends. They are something for which we ought to act. In any case such "aims" limit intelligence; they are not the expression of mind in foresight, observation, and choice of the better among alternative possibilities. They limit intelligence because, given ready-made, they must be imposed by some authority external to intelligence, leaving to the latter nothing but a mechanical choice of means.[5]

These "externally supplied ends" cannot adequately guide practice because they lack the experimental quality that allows their development in response to the educational situation. A sound aim, on the other hand

> surveys the present state of experience of pupils, and forming a tentative plan of treatment, keeps the plan constantly in view and yet modifies it as conditions develop. The aim, in short, is experimental, and hence constantly growing as it is tested in action.[6]

Sound educational aims are not static, rigid, goals in themselves; on the contrary, they are flexible means of guiding, in this case, CSL projects in their communal, service, academic, reflective, and democratic practice.

CSL Aims: A Categorical Treatment

Richard Kraft points out that one "of the major difficulties in evaluating or researching service-learning programs is the lack of agreement on what is meant by the term service-learning and exactly what it is meant to accomplish."[7] CSL certainly is in need of more clearly defined aims, and that clarification can be accomplished only by clarifying its practice: the conceptions of practice I outline in the later chapters imply particular kinds of educational aims, and vice versa—aims and means are inseparable and organically connected. I also want to be clear that the categories of aims that follow are not mutually exclusive; community goals are closely entangled with critical reflective goals; academic aims are intertwined with democratic ends, and so forth. These categories simply represent the means to conceptualize inexorably connected aims that can be reasonably expected in CSL projects.

Finally, a reminder that what follows is a philosophical treatment of CSL aims; that is, I will suggest those educational aims that make sense given its structure and how those aims might practically direct project activities. As to other non-philosophical research that investigates the outcomes of CSL are expansive indeed; in fact, most contemporary CSL research is concerned with outcomes or impacts or goals manifested, or not, in CSL projects. I wonder with Richard Kraft whether such research is sensible sans a discussion of what aims make conceptual sense. On the other hand, it would be a mistake to discount these research findings out of hand. With that in mind, you will find a substantial list of impact research in an appendix at the end of the book, organized in categories, not meant to be exhaustive, but as a starting point for further examination in light of what I suggest below.

Reflective "Critical Thinking"

As I will explain in Chapter Eight, critical reflection, particularly on the part of students and community members, is the impetus for CSL and is the glue that bonds community service activities, classroom academics, and community improvement in a truly viable, truly transformative CSL project. It is reflection, as conceived in Chapter Eight that is the essential practice of CSL; however, reflection is not only the means by which other valued educational aims are pursued, it is an aim of CSL in and of itself. CSL is specifically conceived, at least in part, to develop critical reflective skills and a critically reflective disposition among all project participants; and critical reflection is essential to *each* of the general categories of aims I explain below. As such, reflective thinking is the overarching aim of CSL, but unfortunately, it is regularly underdeveloped in CSL projects.

Reflective thinking first and foremost guides human decision-making when a problem in experience is initially felt. Reflection frees human beings from mere impulse and blind habit in mediating instinctual reaction based on impulse so that a reasonable rather than an unreasonable action decision might be reached. In reflection, impulse is transformed into purpose and freedom is practiced—certainly a core aim of any democratic educational approach. Sound CSL theory and its resulting practice aims to develop the reflective skills as well as the disposition of reflective patience.

In addition to being a dispositional aim of CSL, reflective thinking makes possible the application of purely abstract academic learning in creative and useful ways. A problem cannot be solved without developing and practicing reflective thinking related to solving problems. Nor can academic skills be learned without a strong reflective component. The mathematical order of operations, for example, means little to a student until it is applied through the reflective process to a real problem in experience. CSL aims to develop reflective reasoning by supplying reflective instruction, modeling, and the opportunity to apply solutions deemed viable via the reflective process. Using academic skills through reflective application creates a much deeper understanding of them on the part of the student. Understood from this Deweyan perspective, reflection is an important aim entailed within each and every CSL project, as well as a democratic developmental goal important to finding solutions to broad communal problems. Sans a strong reflective component, CSL projects tend to be "miseducative" experiences.

As a democratic/character development goal that has ramifications beyond the specific CSL project, critical reflection is equally paramount. The freedom of democracy demands thoughtful decisions and responsible action. Without both the ability and inclination to step back and reflect before acting, the result may be unreasonable actions or no action at all. Without a reflective public, democracy stagnates.[8] As a democratic form of education (a case I will make in Chapter Nine), CSL should aim to develop democratic inclinations. Reflection is the core democratic practice and stands as the most important educational aim of CSL in its relationship to the advancement of democracy as both a political system and as a way of living.[9] Additionally as a critical orientation in what I will suggest as a strong version of CSL, the focus of critical reflection on systemically oppressive institutional structures is the most important distinguishing factor between it and the weaker conception of CSL.

Finally, reflection is the essential activity that can transform a community. Until a problem solution is tested through thought and resulting action, it cannot be evaluated and problems cannot be solved. Problems can be solved only if a continual aim of CSL projects is to develop reflective skills and habits. As the core aim, it directs CSL practitioners toward community projects that encourage reflective development. Reflective thinking is clearly an aim that is directive, flexible, and entailed in every step of CSL

Academic Aims

Academic aims are inherent in most, if not all, educational approaches. Educational schemes of every stripe—traditional or progressive, student centered or test driven—demand that students learn to read, write, manipulate numbers, have a working knowledge of important facts, think critically, and so forth. It follows that academic aims are a common area of inquiry for CSL research. It is reasonable to expect any and all educational models to have these basic academic aims. What distinguishes CSL from other educational approaches is the means used to meet those academic goals. Whereas in the more traditional notions of education the emphasis is on memorizing and testing, CSL emphasizes critical thinking and application of skills in authentic experiential contexts: academic skills learned in the classroom are strengthened through applying them to problems in the community. Reflective thinking guides the application of academic skills to solve the community problem. In this way, academic lessons become vitally important tools to the students and are, therefore, more deeply valued and understood.

When academics are used to solve such authentic problems, they must be understood clearly and applied correctly. As tools needed to solve felt difficulties, classroom lessons and their application become important to all project stakeholders. If academics are not understood or their application to the problem is inappropriate, the problem will not be solved. In learning, applying, adjusting, relearning, and reapplying academics, they become lessons that will not be soon forgotten. Academic aims are important guides for choosing and organizing projects—projects that are expected to increase content knowledge and skills.

The example of mathematical order of operations is telling. This relatively simple mathematical rule should be introduced in the "classroom."[10] It can then be applied to the problem situation as part of a broader problem-solution plan. By utilizing that skill in creative and reflective ways, students learn both its potential and its limitations as a tool. In determining what academic skills and knowledge are appropriate to the situation and how they should be appropriately used, those skills become vitally important to the student and are therefore vitally understood. This is a simple example of what was advocated by Kilpatrick, Hanna, and Dewey, as I explained in Chapter Three and take up in greater detail in Chapter Seven. Reflecting on the way academic skill should be used not only enhances understanding, it also advances the overarching aim of critical reflection.

It must be noted here that the way student academic growth is evaluated will establish, to some degree, the status of the aim in question. That is, the evaluation process can partially determine whether or not an academic aim is philosophically sound. In the contemporary educational world of NCLB, where final student evaluation is based on pencil and paper, statewide, standardized tests, the specific academic aims of CSL become problematic. Using a paper-and-pencil test is, in and of itself, not a problem as long as it isn't the one and only indicator of meeting academic aims. That is, a standardized test that evaluates externally supplied aims might be a useful diagnostic tool for a misguided practice.

However, the NCLB-driven assessment practice of high-stakes testing compromises both the ends and means of CSL. Learning to take a test that requires the regurgitation of information presented in lecture form is antithetical to CSL as an educational approach founded in student felt problems and experiential service to others—not to mention its antithetical understanding of what constitutes understanding. These test-established academic aims are exactly the type that John Dewey and other progressive educators warned against: they are rigid and offer teachers only "a mechanical choice of means."[11] Aims that direct practice in CSL must be responsive to the situation at hand, not established without knowledge of that situation. "Testing" in a CSL situation demands that evaluative examinations take into account the specific educational situation and aims and requires broad and varied means of showing what was learned.[12] High-stakes standardized testing does neither and simply eliminates the numerous advantages of CSL.

Advocates of CSL expect that academic growth will not just keep pace, but will outpace more traditional approaches to teaching academics.[13] Academic growth is very much entailed in its practice, particularly when those aims are formulated in a philosophically sound manner. Students should come away from a CSL project with a working knowledge of academic concepts and skills, but also a deeper understanding of that knowledge because of the fact that they initiated interest in solving truly felt problems. Rigorous academic goals are important for directing a successful CSL project and prove it to be anything but a soft pedagogy. In fact, when academic aims guide experiential learning, they will lead students to a depth of understanding that is not possible in traditional modes of teaching and learning.

Democratic Character Aims

Democratic character development, though important in traditional educational approaches, is not emphasized in the traditional context as explicitly as it is in the CSL context. In the numerous definitions and descriptions of CSL mentioned earlier in this study, as well as specific suggestions for practice made by such scholars as Battistoni and Barber, democratic character development maintains a unique and essential role.[14] The democratic application of academic lessons most completely distinguishes CSL from traditional educational approaches. Democratic character development as an educational aim is entailed by CSL in its notion of reflection among all service participants (student, teacher, community member) and in its notion of community service.

It is especially here, that those broad, social questions mentioned above come into play. That is, in order for an educational endeavor to develop democratic character, there must be an understanding of such concepts as democracy, character, responsibility, citizenship, and so on.[15] As will be argued in Chapter Nine, these are issues that need further attention in relationship to CSL. Suffice it to say here that democratic character, as understood in CSL practice, has at least these identifying traits: a willingness to interact with community "strangers"; a willingness to participate in democratic processes such as public debate and public elections; a view of individuals as equal partners in the democratic endeavor, regardless of race, gender, ethnicity, or other cosmetic differences; an inclination to act on reasonable, reflective decisions; the confidence that each individual (particularly oneself) has the ability and responsibility to participate in decision making; and a general ethical disposition toward genuine, caring, and honest debate in making democratic decisions. These dispositions are what Robert Bellah calls democratic "habits of the heart" and are also democratic character aims of CSL.[16]

The habit or disposition toward public debate and participation is, in fact, at the heart of the CSL pedagogy. As I will argue in the coming chapters, viable CSL projects are the result of a felt problem in student experience. That feeling of a community problem is a democratic activity in and of itself. Problem realization is an indication of sensitivity to other individuals as well as the community at large. It's the understanding that all individual community members are needy, in some way or another. Finally, CSL encourages the idea that community needs can be met by working together, particularly so when community is envisioned as I outline it in the next chapter.

Again, reflection focuses student and teacher energy on solving the particular community problem through a reasonable mediation of experience and thoughtful hypothesizing and application of solutions. Reflection on community problems strengthens both the idea and the use of democratic decision and action. Through reflection, students come to understand the importance, in fact the necessity, of solving community problems communally. As Seymour Lipset argued more recently, and Alexis de Tocqueville observed long ago, in a society held together by common creed rather than by common ethnic history, it is through communal association and action that democratic decisions must be made.[17] This is an important lesson to be learned in CSL projects. Finally, action and reevaluation during project work further develops the disposition to democratic action, as solutions to problems are formulated, acted upon, and judged for success. Acting to solve problems of interest on the part of students and teachers opens the possibility for further such action in other future community problem situations—the project is educative.

It is easy to see how proponents of CSL can expect such a wide variety of outcomes even in its weaker form as indicated by the research cited in the appendix. Given a stronger version of CSL, service as understood here (and explained in Chapter Ten) provides nearly limitless opportunities to develop democratic dispositions in participating students. Service also provides nearly limitless opportunities to develop the very specific democratic character that America's political situation demands.

One example from the character outcomes research shows what this character development can mean to a community, especially given a strong version of CSL. Ethnic tolerance and understanding remain issues even today, centuries after the founding of the United States, and is increasingly a focus of CSL scholarship. CSL projects provide the opportunity for ethnic strangers to meet, work together, and solve common community problems. In doing so, the barriers among strangers fade and systemic oppression might be eased. The crucial understanding that individuals from different ethnic groups have more in common than they have differences emerges quickly after the CSL project work begins. Cooperative interaction rather than divisiveness is the key to solving perceived community problems. The specific problem of ethnic understanding is attacked and in so doing, the general democratic character traits noted above are developed in the specific project activities; and once again, the general reflective habit of mind is continually developed and improved. Claims that CSL projects can transform these kinds of community attitudes are supported by both research and philosophical analysis. And again, given a strong notion of CSL, transformations beyond those of self are conceivable: transformations of existing institutional structures are potentially possible.

Though more traditional approaches to education in the United States advocate character education, it is not necessarily entailed in the educational process. For example, several states have adopted a program entitled "Character Counts" to teach democratic morality. Each month a different character "pillar" is emphasized (for example, truth, loyalty, care). Generally, that emphasis comes in the form of lectures, posters, bumper stickers, and other advertising-like schemes. Teachers are expected to emphasize the particular pillar each month. Clearly, this is the kind of aim John Dewey warned against. Not only is the aim imposed from outside of the educational context, it is also delivered to students rather than learned in experience.

CSL, on the other hand, has democratic character as a built-in aim: it's entailed in its practice. Using academic skills and reflective thinking in active problem solving develops general democratic character as students interact with one another in their community. The shift in focus from simply talking and reading about democracy, to actually doing democracy, makes the character-development aim a philosophically reasonable one in well-conceptualized and practiced CSL projects.

Community Transformation Aims

The final general category of CSL aims is that of community transformation. It is clearly the most removed from traditional public-school aims that tend to isolate schools from a community and its problems. Rather than be a source for problem solution, public schools are often seen as the source of those problems. CSL aims, however, demand that a school operate as an integral and active democratic community institution. Paul Hanna's discussion nearly 75 years ago provides the clearest and most complete understanding of how CSL activities can and should foster democracy in a community. Hanna's argument was that when students and teachers leave the school and enter the community at large, they necessarily transform both community and school in important democratic ways. The trick, according to Hanna, is to ensure that the impact is positive and truly transformative. That is, the betterment of the entire community is the aim of community transformative action and must be clearly and continually kept in mind.

Specifically, Hanna suggested that a service project must meet three criteria to be acceptable and socially valuable. The first of these is that:

> Any project must culminate in the actual improvement of living in the community. Only when proposals are effective in changing the environment for the better can they be considered satisfactory from a pragmatic viewpoint. Further, the world is so desperately in need of action for improvement that intelligent leadership of the young cannot permit the youthful energies to be dulled by endless discussion about action.[18]

Hanna's point, though made many years ago, remains important for contemporary CSL theory and its implementation. If a CSL project does not have as one of its goals the resolution of a felt community problem, then the project is doomed from the outset. This does not mean that every community problem attacked by a CSL project will be solved on the first attempt. Reflective, human activity simply does not work this efficiently. However, it does mean that in successive attempts to devise and act on a problem in experience, the aim of solving that problem must be continually emphasized. If community-service activity descends to merely social activity, CSL is no longer a viable democratic practice. Without the guiding aim of solving a problem, project activity becomes inauthentic and runs the danger of teaching anti-democratic rather than democratic dispositions. Thought, without action, in Hanna's argument, is not in any sense educational. That is, felt difficulties must be acted on with community improvement as the aim or else the work becomes the worst form of abstraction and undemocratic.

Secondly, Hanna suggested that though there clearly are some issues for which adults must take responsibility, and others that students might be disposed to deal with, it's best that adults and young people work together in solving the community problem. In his words, "Projects must clearly be an obligation of youth as well as adulthood."[19] Youth must see that community problem-solving is a responsibility for them as well as for adults. That goal can be accomplished best by organizing projects cooperatively on the part of both teacher and student. With this criterion of community impact, it is easy to see how democratic character development and community transformation go hand in hand. Through cooperative democratic work, service learning changes the community—not only by solving problems, but also by developing young people who will continue to work for community improvement. This type of communal work perpetuates the idea that all community members are responsible for its wellbeing—a "freedom to" perspective on community life, which I take up more completely in the next chapter. It is a philosophical position that encourages a growing democratic confidence in young people—a confidence that will carry through to adult life. Social activity to solve current community problems, not simply to prepare for them in some future adult life, should be the goal of any CSL project. When done well, this aim is necessarily entailed in CSL practice.

Finally, and possibly most importantly, CSL projects should aim to bring about fundamental community change:

> In so far as possible, projects must get at the basic problems of improving social welfare. Projects must not contribute to the further entrenchment of a social practice which is obviously evil. As an illustration: a project of providing Thanksgiving baskets for the poor, while lessening suffering for the moment, does not get at the root of the evil: the inadequate income of the majority of our families. Not only may the Thanksgiving-baskets-for-the-poor type of project contribute to the notion that we should hold a class of citizens in economic slavery in order that those of us who are more fortunate may annually have the smug satisfaction of "sharing" but, in addition, time and energy given to such superficial betterment could much more effectively be spent in getting at the basic inhibiting influences which perpetuate a scarcity-economy in the midst of abundance. Probably no other criterion in the social category is more often violated by project leaders who intend to do the best possible thing for youth and society, but fail to see that the project really contributes little even to the immediate amelioration of the evil and may even further crystallize it. If project leaders would guide the planning phases of projects more carefully and thoroughly and, through research and experimentation, drive the roots to deeper soil, many projects which have been insignificant might be made significant in community improvement.[20]

This very important aspect of community impact speaks directly to how service is conceived and practiced and hints at what might be entailed in strong CSL. The point here is that the project work should create a fundamentally reconstructed community situation. A deep and lasting solution as well as deep and abiding social connections should be the goal of CSL projects for them to satisfy community improvement, self-reconstruction, and democratic character aims. This deep and lasting community relationship will transform the individuals involved in the project; at the same time, the deep and lasting problem-solution will transform the entire community. The democratic community impact aim has to be conceived as a permanent one in both the server-served relationships, as well as in the actual problem-solution. Again, if this aim is not kept at the forefront of project activities, the project itself, as Hanna suggests, could worsen the problem and create further class division, rather than stronger democratic connections required by CSL community aims.

Implicit in these three criteria is the idea that essential school/community relationships must be established and strengthened. William Kilpatrick argued that these kinds of community projects ultimately "Serve to bring the youthful group (school or church or club, etc.) into desirable intimate contact with the surrounding community."[21] Clearly this must be a continual community impact aim in any CSL project. In the final analysis, having students successfully participate in solving community problems builds a confidence among adults that young people are not just the cause of problems, but instead can provide the solutions. It also reassures students that adults have student welfare in mind when they act to solve community problems because those students work side by side with adults to solve the problems. It creates a school that is intimately connected to the broader community and strengthens democracy.

Implications for Practice

To summarize, educational aims must be entailed in practice and not placed onto practice externally. CSL goals fall into three categories: academics, character development, and community impact. Adding the overarching goal and practice of reflective thinking makes CSL aims complete and understandable: the goals of academic growth, character development, and community transformation are sound aims when CSL practice is clearly understood. When aims of CSL are established from within its practice, adjusted during practice, and continually guide that practice, the full power of the CSL pedagogy is plain to see. Its expectations go well beyond those found in traditional pedagogical approaches that emphasize lecture, memorization, and abstraction.

When these aims are understood as entailed in its practice, CSL is an educational reform that in its weak form is much more than the soft pedagogy decried in years gone by. In its strong form, CSL might radically change schools and their relationships to community. In either version, CSL is an approach that is much more difficult for a teacher to organize and implement. It means that she must be sensitive to the developmental characteristics of her students so that aims, particularly academic and democratic aims, can be appropriately established. It means that a teacher must be flexible in adjusting aims as new situations and discoveries are made. Finally, and most removed from traditional practice, she must be clear that the school is an important interactive community institution and her students are vital players in its community role. The teacher, therefore, must continually develop her own sense of the community and adjust that understanding as her students transform it. She has to be clear in teaching her students that they are part of the community, particularly its problems and their solutions. When practiced as suggested in this study, CSL can reach each of these categorical goals as project work weaves together academic, democratic, and critical development in solving community problems and growing school-community relationships.

As a final note on aims, the degree and type of goals that can be achieved in CSL projects is directly correlated with the degree to which the projects are weak or strong versions of CSL— correlated to where they fall on a weak/strong continuum. That place on the weak/strong continuum can, I believe, be understood in the degree to which projects remain, simply, supporters of democratic institutional structures, and the degree to which they critically interrogate such institutional structures. That is ultimately a matter of focus and comes out of initially understanding CSL as a democratic educational endeavor. But before getting to the specific distinctions between weak and strong, we must more completely draw out the conceptions of community, service, experiential learning, reflection, and their implications for practice.

CHAPTER FIVE

Community: A Rose by Any Other Name...

Introduction

I grew up in a time and place that honored the family meal—a practice that served, I now believe, as a bulwark against a growing (some would say "post-modern") splintering of family and communal life evidenced by a seemingly infinite number of overly organized, overly scheduled, overly institutionalized, and overly inorganic activities for children, and a simultaneous reduction in civic participation among adults. Today, many families rarely have the time or energy to sit down for a meal together, given there is homework to be done and organized practices to be gotten to (and gotten to "on time"), much less the time to participate in civic organizations. It is telling that even the free play of young children has turned into organized "play dates" and the days of a neighborhood pick-up game of basketball has given way to meticulously planned practices pitting players against players and teams against teams—all done to give my child a leg-up on your child. At the risk of waxing nostalgic, I think these are signs of a shift in communal living that is increasingly based on selfish individualism run amuck—an individualism evidenced by the relatively recent explosion of gated communities and our growing habit of "bowling alone"—an individualism lacking the ruggedness of days gone by.[1]

My mother and father saw the family meal as the means to catch up on the day's activities; deal with any problems; talk over newsworthy events; argue over matters of fact (I have fond memories of my father running over to our collection of Encyclopedia Britannica to settle issues usually brought up by my older sister); and, it seems, as a perfect time for Dad to show off his working knowledge of Shakespearean quotes to a captive audience. His all

time favorite was Polonius' advice to Laertes on the value of "neither a beggar nor borrower be"—one he regularly turns to even
now. Another of his regulars was Juliet's philosophical inquiry
into what impact names have on human experience: "What's in a
name? That which we call a rose by any other name would smell
as sweet." My response to Juliet, well, maybe—at least for the
objects of experience, but maybe not so much when it comes to socially constructed conceptual understandings.

If you peruse the large number of publications on CSL, you will
see several derivations of CSL: "service learning," "service-
learning," "community service-learning," "traditional service learning," "community service learning," "critical service-learning" and,
I'm sure, others I have yet to run across. My decision to use *community* service learning rather than any of the others is done with
purpose: I name community because I believe there is a particular
conception of community that both supports the CSL pedagogy and
that is entailed in its practice; I name community because understanding it is essential to CSL's practice—equally essential as the
concepts service and learning implied in its community practice.
CSL, by any other name, may smell as sweet, but may not be understood well enough to meet its educational and communal potential.

I will also remind us that the progressive tradition as outlined
in Chapter Three conceives community in two associated ways
with respect to schools: first, the school is a community in and of
itself—a fact so universally understood as to be hardly worth mentioning, though certainly implicated in a school's practice as a
community. Second, schools are (or should be) an integral part of
the broader community rather than marked off from it. It is this
second notion of community that is often given lip service by educational policymakers and school administrators but seldom appears in actual school practice—PNS being a rare example of a
school fully integrated into the life of the community—and it is
this second notion that is essential to CSL.

In CSL projects, the typical separation of school and community decried by progressive educators is necessarily erased, since its
practice specifically requires schools to actively engage in the solving of broad communally felt problems. However, as Paul Hanna
explained, community-service projects will meet their communally
transformative potential only when they provide something

beyond a temporary cosmetic Band-aid solution to the problem—community transformation comes in solving problems rather than temporarily easing their symptoms—and CSL so conceived can, I believe, accomplish just that.

I also want to push the envelope here just a bit and echo what George Counts suggested schools might provide communities and hint a bit at what I will later suggest is a strong version of CSL. In *Dare the School Build a New Social Order?* (my short response to that is "yes"), Counts argues that schools should be about more than simply "contemplating civilization," they should be actively "building civilization."[2] CSL, as a communally transforming pedagogy, can and should do just that—CSL projects thus conceived are reflective of Counts' somewhat radicalized progressive sentiment, Paul Hanna's belief in community-service projects that go beyond mere temporary fixes, and the social-justice notion championed in more contemporary critical theory outlined earlier. In this way, both project participants and the community are truly transformed.

There was a time when I believed CSL had only limited potential as a democratic educational reform—pedagogically valuable, but limited in its broader impact—a weak version of the pedagogy. In some ways I still buy that argument (and I discuss it as such in a later chapter). However, I am increasingly convinced that CSL has valuable radical potential as a reconstructive educational revolution of sorts—individually, institutionally, communally, and educationally—when understood from Counts' activist perspective. (I take this up near the end of the book.) However, lest I get ahead of myself, understanding CSL as either a reform or a revolution turns, at least initially, on the community theory it embraces; and the conception of community entailed in CSL, I believe, turns on an issue most often taken up by political philosophers: the nature of human liberty.

Liberty: "Freedom From" or "Freedom To?"

The nature of human liberty or freedom (I use these interchangeably) has long been a topic of social, political, and philosophical inquiry, especially so within the context of democracy. One of the better-known philosophically technical discussions—one that distinguishes between negative and positive liberty—is contained in a lecture delivered in 1958 by Isaiah Berlin. Berlin's explanation of the distinction is clear, succinct, and has obvious implications for the concept and practice of community entailed in CSL.

Berlin writes that under the "freedom from" notion of negative liberty:

> I am normally said to be free to the degree to which no human being interferes with my activity. Political liberty in this sense is simply the area within which a man can do what he wants. If I am prevented by other persons from doing what I want, I am to that degree unfree; and if the area within which I can do what I want is contracted by other men beyond a certain minimum, I can be described as being coerced, or, it may be, enslaved.[3]

Positive liberty, or the "freedom to" conception, on the other hand, entails something beyond just the freedom from coercion. Berlin writes:

> The "positive" sense of the word "liberty" derives from the wish on the part of the individual to be his own master. I wish my life and decisions to depend on myself, not on external forces of whatever kind. I wish to be the instrument of my own, not of other men's, acts of will. I wish to be a subject, not an object; to be moved by reasons, by conscious purposes which are my own, not by causes which affect me, as it were, from outside. I wish to be somebody, not nobody; a doer—deciding, not being decided for, self-directed and not acted upon by external nature or by other men as if I were a thing, or an animal, or a slave incapable of playing a human role, that is, of conceiving goals and policies of my own and realizing them.[4]

At first glance, the distinction between "freedom from" and "freedom to" seems minor at best, but upon closer analysis the two entail quite different notions of community.

The key to the communal difference entailed in positive versus negative notions of freedom is found in the implications positive liberty has for the envisioning and development of "self." Positive liberty, as explained by Berlin, accounts for human agency; it distinguishes humans from "animals" and "slaves" in that it entails human choice—choice that engenders a sense of self that can play "a human role." Positive liberty implies an individualism that goes beyond simply being free from coercion, something deeper than simply the right to do whatever one wants sans concerns for how choice plays out in human undertakings. It is a conception of freedom that goes beyond the simple restriction against limiting the liberty of others. Positive liberty implies a development of self that is communal, an accomplishing of individual human aspirations that can only be achieved through community rather than in exclusion or absolution from it.

In an understanding of freedom that is negative, I have the right to do what I please as long as it does not limit that same right for other individuals. Positive liberty, however, suggests that though I have that same right, I also have an obligation to be mindful of how my acting on that right impacts those around me, beyond whether it limits the freedom of other individuals. This is an obligation to the various communities of which I am a part and that have been essential in my development of self.

In, *Teaching the Commons*, an insightful book on the historic decay of rural communities, Paul Theobald argues that the shift from a positive to a negative understanding of freedom is sourced in a gradual rejection of intradependence and adoption of a radical independence:

> Throughout most of human history, people lived their lives in a given locality and were highly dependent on the place itself and on those others with whom the place was shared. It has only been since the seventeenth century or so that intradependence of this sort has eroded and people have begun to think of themselves as individuals unencumbered by the constraints of nature or community. "Freedom" was the term we used to describe our unencumbered lives. Prior to this time, the definition of freedom was not so easily divorced from the entanglement of mutual obligations.[5]

This radical independence, or as I termed it earlier, individualism run amuck, has evolved as a general shift to understanding freedom in the negative sense explained by Berlin. As Theobald says:

> Negative freedom is the "freedom from" coercion, or being told what one can and cannot do. Positive freedom is the "freedom to" maximize the personal development that accrues from shouldering responsibility in a web of social relations. Negative freedom is individual based; positive freedom is community based. In other words, freedom is not that which enables us to walk away from our home or our job (negative freedom), but rather is that which allows us to do those things that give joy and meaning to our lives (positive freedom).[6]

I suggested at the outset of this chapter that CSL entails, and then works to foment, a particular vision of community. This communal understanding as either a democratic reform or a radical revolution is, as Theobald suggests, in part a return to the communal practice witnessed by Alexis de Tocqueville in his visits to our fledgling democracy—a version of community sourced in a freedom-to understanding of human liberty wherein individual goals are accomplished most satisfactorily via community; and community goals are most satisfactorily accomplished through forming associations and building communities of interest, with individuals typically moving across those communities of interest in continual re-association. In what follows, I will first take up in more detail what I believe is entailed by CSL in terms of a community theory, and then, its practical implications for both community- and self-development.

The Liberalism-Communitarianism Debate

I promised I would not lead us down the sometimes-inescapable rabbit hole of philosophical abstraction, and I won't. On the other hand, I think it is valuable to summarize some of the morass that has developed around questions of individualism and communalism. The implications of the distinction between the freedom from and the freedom to conceptions of liberty outlined above have been playing out in debates among political philosophers and economists for quite some time. These debates have generally been between those who embrace enlightenment-sourced liberalism and those who embrace more communal notions of individual agency, historically found in Marxist thought, socialist politics, and more recently in communitarianism.

Liberalism is essentially, though to varying degrees, based on the enlightenment idea that an individual human being has both the wherewithal and the right to make decisions completely free of coercion—a freedom from worldview. Early liberalism was truly revolutionary and resulted in the equally revolutionary political-system-in-practice: democracy—the democracy that Tocqueville saw playing out in American communities early in our history. The idea that individuals can make a life of their own choosing may seem a bit blasé to us moderns, but given that it came against the backdrop of feudalism wherein one's place in life was completely determined by parents and place, it was truly revolutionary and became the basis for the myth of the American Dream.

The concern that communitarian-oriented scholars have with classical liberalism is that it has (as I suggested above) run amuck. The historic orientation that individual actors have had toward the outward, toward other individuals, and toward community, argue the communitarians, has been supplanted with an inward orientation of introspection, individualism, and, some would say, a rather vehement form of particularly American narcissism. As I previously suggested, I think there is ample evidence of this unrestrained American version of selfish individualism.

The "rugged individualism" of our early history, on the other hand—a stubborn attitude that supported a difficult life on the frontiers of this new world—was replete with the understanding that one's very survival depended not only on that individual strength, but that strength in concert with, and in support of, other individual actors. The individualism that conquered both nature and natives in, admittedly, some horrible acts against both, was driven by individualism, but accomplished communally. The settling of the frontier combined with the mind-boggling progress in the production and control of material things has eroded that rugged individualism and in its place has slowly evolved a new individualism oriented toward selfish materialism, nicely captured in that well-known bumper sticker: "whoever dies with the most toys wins!"

On the other hand, classic liberalism does have something important to preserve in its suggestion, and concomitant demand, that individual human beings have the right and the capacity to direct their own lives as they see fit. The danger that classical liberal thinkers rightly see is that individual conceptions of what constitutes the good life can be quickly and easily subsumed, rather than communally and democratically accounted for, by the "borg-like" corporate-ness found in communitarian theory and practice.

Communitarian scholars such as Alasdair MacIntyre, Charles Taylor, and Amitai Etzioni give themselves away on this count, so to speak, in what I believe is a communitarian form of doublethink. They seem able to hold the belief in individual choice while severely limiting one's options or in demonizing individual choice in predetermining the limits/scope of choice. Charles Taylor, in his important discussion *The Malaise of Modernity* writes of "significant horizons" that lie outside of the individual as chooser; horizons communally "given" rather than reasonably decided upon; horizons that are significant in that the "choosing" within these significant horizons has import and impact on both the individual and the community, and the options within these horizons of value are, it seems, determined wholly communally. Ironically, the particular case that Taylor suggests as an important horizon is in the choice of homosexuality.[7]

In much the same way, Etzioni suggests in *Spirit of the Community* that communitarians have no particular positions on what constitutes the good life, and then goes on to quite grievously attack the feminist movement (even women, he chides, have the right to "pursue greed"), and champions the raising of children in a traditional family.[8] MacIntyre's vision, on the other hand, couches communitarian theory in a distinctly religious vision of moral virtue that, in a rather Hegelian way, humans ought to be communally moving toward.[9] The problem that classically leaning liberals point to is of no small import: contemporary communitarians have pre-established notions of the good life with little real regard for individual agency, much less an understanding of the importance of rugged individualism. In each case above, I am reminded of yet another of my father's regular Shakespearean quotes, "The Lady doth protest too much, methinks."

At the risk of making John Dewey out to be overly omniscient (I often wish he would have left at least a couple of stones unturned), he saw that the dualism of individual and community demonstrated in the contemporary liberalism-communitarianism debate held the same dangers as other philosophic and social dualisms and made equally little pragmatic sense.[10] Echoing the sentiments of his colleague George Herbert Mead, Dewey reminds us that

> assured and integrated individuality is the product of definite social rela-
> tionships and publicly acknowledged functions.... If his ideas and beliefs
> are not the spontaneous function of a communal life in which he shares,
> a seeming consensus will be secured as a substitute by artificial and me-
> chanical means.[11]

That is, to suggest that an individual self can come into being, much less make individual decisions and take actions regarding the good life, sans community, is, in the words of my mentor Rob Sherman, "plain silly." Equally silly is the idea that community aspirations and goals can be met, community problems solved, sans the understanding that communal progress is driven by the felt problems of individual community members. Selves are created communally; communities are created in the interaction of individual actors. This relational understanding, I believe, points us toward a reasonable understanding of community that is entailed in and supported by CSL.

Additionally, and importantly for increasingly stronger conceptions of CSL, in the relational development of self via community, more contemporary critical theorists find the source for the construction and institutionalization of oppressive structures and belief systems. Very much related to what I will talk about in more progressive-oriented terms of the internal/external locus, critical theorists suggest that when external exploitation is combined with internal self-discipline—the internalizing of the generalized (typically economic) "other"—that oppression or domination can and typically will go unchecked. Marcuse went so far as to suggest that as capitalism matures, this repression must be redoubled as it smacks in the very face of the human desire for freedom.

Such redoubling, Marcuse argued, is only successful when it becomes a form of internal self-repression, what he termed "surplus repression."[12] Through a process of "repressive desublimation," Marcuse explains that we learn to happily trade political freedom for the ability to buy those toys touted in the above-mentioned bumper sticker, thereby participating in our own repression.[13] As I said earlier, I have a love-hate relationship with critical theorists, and this is a perfect example. More simply put, vehement individualism dupes us into believing we are autonomously free because we can succeed in the market place, when in fact what we are really buying is a form of repression that we ourselves support from within an understanding of the freedom from notion of liberty.

Again, I think this sentiment is accurately reflective of the contemporary context (once the mysterious language is unraveled, it is quite helpful) and is evidenced by a vehement consumerism and an atrophied democracy—one in which civic participation has been replaced with an individualism no longer rugged, but selfish, consumerist, and without compassion for other community members. It is an individualism run amuck. I believe critically strong CSL projects can erode this selfish individualism and challenge oppressive institutional structures that are internalized as self-repressive ideologies. However, as I suggest below, developing the rugged individualism required for first seeing and then challenging such oppressive structures, can only be accomplished with a reconstructed notion of community—one that is grounded in democratic, pragmatic, and liberal notions of community and self, and one that is skeptical of objective scientism.

Toward a "Grown-up" Democratically Pragmatic Liberal Understanding of Community

What I will argue for here is a conception of community sourced in an evolved liberalism—a "grown-up" version of classical liberalism—one deeply indebted to Dewey's renascent liberalism, akin to Barbara Thayer-Bacon's "relational pluralistic democracy always-in-the-making" and similar to what I have called simply "democratic pluralism."[14] I will take up this conception of liberalism one step at a time, one concept at a time, one name at a time, and with a reminder: I am suggesting a *community* theory here, not a full-blown theory of democracy, though certainly democracy is an essential aspect of it.[15] As a community theory, it reflects my belief that democracy grows out of community, and not vice versa. Democratic institutions such as public and/or private schools are viable only in so far as they serve various communities of interest, which, I believe, are the vehicle by which individual visions of what constitutes the good life can be rationally considered and communally achieved.

Liberalism

I will work my way through this in reverse order, as I think the essential anchor of my suggestion is found in a reconstructed understanding of the liberal individual. What I want to save in terms of classical liberalism is the old-style rugged individualism seen early in our history and that is required in John Dewey's renascent liberalism (and one I think Thayer-Bacon gives short shrift). Dewey argues that the fallacy of classic liberalism relative to the individual, particularly a rugged individual, is the a priori belief that individuals "have a full-blown psychological and moral nature, having its own set laws, independently of their association with one another."[16] Dewey suggests that a rugged individualism can only develop in an association between individuals and institutions that encourages and thereby internalizes the habits of mind necessary to foment this form of individualism. Classical liberalism supposed that such associations "were thought of as things that operate from without, not entering in any significant way into the internal make-up or growth of individuals. Social arrangements were treated not as positive forces but as external limitations."[17] In fact, Dewey claims in *Individualism Old and New* that absent such vital interplay, the result is conformity and support for the status quo—the antithesis of the rugged individualism required for social change, if not social progress.[18]

It is at this point that more communitarian-oriented thinkers would suggest that the kind of individualism Dewey is describing is exactly that which ultimately devolves into the narcissistic, selfish individualism decried by me early in this chapter and decried by communitarians regularly. However, I believe Dewey has his finger on something important here. It certainly is in association that individuals internalize particular dispositions of thought and action. On the other hand, communitarianism (or corporate-ness, as Dewey conceived it) in its pre-established dogmatic horizons of belief, leads to an internalization that subsumes individualism to such a degree as to eliminate their rugged-ness thereby maintaining the status quo and retarding progress. The growth hoped for by progressives is, in the end, only accomplished when human and institutional association encourages the internalizing of the rugged individual—one willing to push boundaries, particularly when those boundaries are oppressive, and one willing to stand up to other individuals who are unreasonably oppressive. The communitarian, on the other hand, might feel quite threatened by such individualism.

Before I move on to the pragmatic aspect of my thinking here, a question is certainly begged: what is meant by rugged individualism in light of contemporary circumstances? I think the best way to address that question is by providing a couple of examples from recent history. Two examples that immediately come to mind (certainly there are numerous others) is the Civil Rights movement of last century and an ongoing contemporary civil rights movement related to our public schools. I find it nearly impossible to think of the Civil Rights movement of the 1960s without the names Rosa Parks, Martin Luther King, Jr. and Malcolm X immediately coming to mind; nor is it possible for me to think about the fight against the tragic resegregation of public schools over the last several decades without thinking of Jonathan Kozol. There is a reason for that: these are clearly instances of the prototypical rugged individual committing acts of reasonable political community activism—"selves" developed in their associations with other selves, communities of interest, and institutions such that a rugged unwillingness to abide the status quo has been internalized to the point of acting. This aspect of liberal individualism is, I believe, both worth preserving and entailed in CSL.

The Pragmatic

I use the term pragmatic here to point us toward Thayer-Bacon's concern with Dewey's (and others) naïve faith in science as the arbiter of truth and the silliness entailed in an either-or understanding of community and self. Again, working backward, George Herbert Mead, in his seminal work, *Mind, Self, and Society*, put this self/community dualism to final rest in suggesting that there can be no sense of individual self without a communally generated "generalized other." Without the generalized other, there can be no conception of self in its relation to others.[19] Nor can there be individual "originality of thought."[20]

A less silly question in terms of the pragmatic aspect of this community thinking is Thayer-Bacon's desire to eliminate "rationalism" from our democratic undertaking, by which she means Dewey's strict reliance on the scientific, experimental method.[21] In an ensuing chapter I will, in greater detail, discuss the experimental epistemology that pragmatists suggest is essential to determining issues of knowledge and even truth with particular attention to CSL. For now, my concern on this count can be characterized by that old saying, "throwing the baby out with the bathwater."

Thayer-Bacon suggests that feminist and critical theorists have shown that science itself is impacted by socially constructed paradigm shifts that make science less than rational. Critical and feminist theorists certainly have been pointing this out, and reasonably so.[22] I think, however, the idea that science is subjective and creative was made much earlier by various quantum physicists and powerfully by Thomas Kuhn in his *Structure of Scientific Revolutions*.[23] In any case, by all accounts, science, the experimental method, has a distinctively creative aspect to it. The problem with Dewey's acceptance of the scientific method, hook, line, and sinker, particularly as it is seen from our postmodern perspective, has to do with his hope that it could mediate subjectivity and in its place, posit a form of objectivity. Dewey's naïveté is the naïveté of the modern—he was a person of his time; on the other hand, our postmodern skepticism holds the danger of a debilitating hopelessness.

I think we can find a safe middle ground in a version of Dewey's experimentalism tempered by the understanding expressed in contemporary critical theory of all kinds: at the end of the day, objectivity is a mythical idea akin to the unicorn. Even science, and maybe especially science, is a creative, subjective, endeavor. Rather than discard rationalism whole hog, in embracing both experimentalism's scientific and aesthetic nature, I believe we can find and create more pragmatic meaning while deconstructing those historic, supposedly objective truths so often used to oppress rather than to liberate.

The Democratic

I use "democratic" here in the Deweyan sense: democracy is much more than simply a political procedure; it is an associated way of living. I also use it to capture, in this sense, what Thayer-Bacon calls the "relational," and as she rightly points out, the "transactional" of Dewey's later thought. Democracy as such contains a rather large dose of individual, institutional, and community interaction—the kind of interactional or transactional processes that is reflective of Mead's understanding of self and communal creation. Much of this is implied in my earlier discussion.

However, I also use the democratic to answer the communitarian concern that, sans a fully established set of horizons or what I would call pre-established moralisms, there exists no generalized other from which selves can be developed—nothing, that is, to "believe in." What I have elsewhere called democratic pluralism, here I call simply, the democratic:

> a state of society in which members of diverse ethnic, racial, religious, or social groups maintain participation in and development of their traditional culture or special interest while fully participating in democratic decision making through democratic institutions thereby maintaining or creating democratic connections amongst and between those groups.[24]

I have also suggested elsewhere a particular metaphorical understanding of this relational, transactional version of community wherein all communities of interest are vitally important, as relational communities, to a democratically beautiful conception of community. This rather stout (or strong or deep if you prefer) understanding of relational democracy answers the communitarian complaint in that it holds great value as an anti-oppressive horizon of belief. This understanding is vitally entailed and supported in CSL projects that are sourced in individually felt problems, and transformed by the work of rugged individuals into communally felt problems, and then addressed rationally via communal activism. In doing the projects, rugged individualism, communal connection, subjective rationality, and democracy itself can be extended through the institution of P–12 schooling. As I will argue in a later chapter, when based on this understanding of community, CSL is the epitome of a democratic form of education and the basis for a strong conception of CSL.

Before climbing out of this brief rabbit hole of abstraction, a quick word on the charge that Dewey (and more contemporary folks such as Paul Theobald) was impractically nostalgic in his suggestion that only in more agrarian-oriented "neighborly communities" can this conception be supported and accomplished. I do suspect Dewey was overly romantic on this count, particularly later in his career.[25] On the other hand (and I don't spend the time on this question that it warrants), I think it's good to remember that while some communities entail a sense of place, others do not entail a finite place or space. Given advances in technology and the shrinking nature of the world, though communities limited in place will never be eliminated, increasingly they will be supplanted by communities of interest.

Implications for Practice

The notion of community I outline here has some rather powerful implications for teachers and schools engaged in CSL. The core implication and the one most difficult for teachers operating from a more traditional perspective, and certainly made more difficult by NCLB, is that teachers engaged in projects such as those suggested throughout this book, must abdicate much of their power. If, as I have suggested here, we want to develop young, rugged individuals who are willing to act communally against institutional and cultural constructs of oppression, then we as teachers must give individual students and communities of students much freer rein—both in school-as-community and out of school, in the broader community. The traditional authority of the teacher must be transformed into rational guidance (and this will be a theme reinforced more specifically later).

Second, schools have to envision themselves as vital community resources; as was the case with PNS, family and communal life must be brought into the school, and school life into the family/community. In the blurring of the school/community distinction through CSL projects, schools will inevitably see themselves as George Counts hoped: as builders of civilization rather than simple contemplators of civilization. In that blurring of the school/community division, rugged-individual selves will develop against the backdrop of the communal generalized other through democratic social action.

Third, and implied in the teacher-as-guide concept, teachers have to find ways to imbue a sensitivity to community and its problems—large and small—into our students (as progressive educators have suggested, and referenced in the previous chapter). It is only in the degree to which individuals are sensitive to community problems (both communities of place and communities of interest) that individually felt problems can develop into social action to solve said problems. As I suggest later, this will entail not only the growth of self as self, but also a growth of self as an academic endeavor entailed in broadly interdisciplinary studies of past and contemporary culture.

Fourth, the notion of community outlined here entails the development of what Robert Bellah, et al., generally describe as democratic "habits of the heart." I suspect, in fact, that it entails a rather major revitalizing of the American spirit. In a later chapter I will take up these dispositions in more detail. Suffice it to say here that the above understanding of community implies the dispositional encouragement toward critical open-mindedness, communal deliberation, reflective participation, and above all, a sense of compassion for "the other." Lacking these, community as it is envisioned here is simply unsustainable.

Finally (at least for now), if it is the case that individually and communally felt problems are to be eased or solved reasonably and sans further oppression of people and nature, a kinder, gentler

understanding of experimentalism should be at the heart of academic endeavors. The experimentalism that I suggest here must
be mindful of Thayer-Bacon's conception that science (or reason)
does not imply pure objectivity. Students should learn that the
hallmark of human experience is emotion and that even science
has a subjective flavor to it. And that is as it should be. Lacking
this subjective understanding, science, or experimentalism, is void
of the most crucial human qualities—qualities essential to solving
community problems experienced by living, breathing, suffering
human beings and nature, to which we are inexorably connected
and reliant upon.

I have outlined the broad implications that community theory
has on actual implementation of CSL projects. I'll return to these
themes from time to time as I take up the other conceptual components of CSL. And so, back to our original query: "What's in a
name?" Next, I will address the service component in CSL to see
what might come of its practice as a communally and individually
transformative pedagogy.

CHAPTER SIX

Service: Self and Stranger

Introduction

Though the incorporation of specific "service" requirements into schools in the United States (i.e., CSL and other such programs) is a relatively new practice, the general conception of community service is deeply rooted in our history—the history of a new nation constructed around the revolutionary idea of democracy. As I mentioned in Chapters Three and Four, the famed French chronicler of American life, Alexis de Tocqueville, argued that the community service he commonly witnessed in early-19th-century America developed from the political realities of our young democracy and was a core defense against the return of tyranny.[1] Robert Bellah, et al., describe Tocqueville's observation that through

> Active involvement in common concerns, the citizen can overcome the sense of relative isolation and powerlessness that results from the insecurity of life in an increasingly commercial society. Associations along with decentralized local administration mediate between the individual and the centralized state. Associational life, in Tocqueville's thinking, is the best bulwark against the condition he feared most: the mass society of mutually antagonistic individuals, easy prey to despotism.[2]

Thus the political demands of democracy—combined with the philosophical/religious beliefs[3] of the American founders and the physical difficulties of the new frontier—brought about the development of a uniquely American service ethic that remains, at least conceptually, an important aspect of American character, American community, and American political health. Helping one another in times of need was and is an essential activity for the survival of a vibrant democracy. Additionally, this uniquely American service ethic filled the void of lost connections born from our rejection of aristocracy and our embrace of democracy—in our transition from a people held together by a common history, to a people living by a common creed.[4]

Though the general notion of service that Tocqueville observed in America's infancy remains, the particulars of the concept have quite naturally evolved, as our nation has evolved, and now include a variety of "service" activities grounded in a variety of service conceptions including philanthropy, obligation, charity, volunteerism, punishment, and mutuality, among others. As I have argued in previous chapters, ever-evolving philosophical conceptions such as community service can quickly and easily grow out of control and result in confused and/or ineffective (educational) practices if these conceptions are not periodically revisited and reconceptualized. And, as I also suggested previously, I believe that the conception of service commonly practiced in CSL has become over-extended and muddied to the point of confusion. This confusion has lead to less-than-sound CSL practice based on individualism run amok, and is in need of some reclarification. To that end, I argue in this chapter that a philosophically sound and practically useful conception of community service might be constructed that captures both the communal spirit outlined in Chapter Five and the educational goals of CSL based on the work of several scholars, most prominently that of Howard Radest.[5]

Oppressive Notions of Service

A helpful first step in clarifying and then constructing a conception of service that most reasonably supports CSL, is to delineate how service *should not* be conceptualized and then practiced in CSL. Service clearly cannot be identified with the notions of philanthropy, charity, or noblesse oblige found in the American poorhouse tradition. Each of these, though slightly different conceptually, are one sided, ultimately oppressive attempts to help the "lost," "lonely" and "needy" of the neighborhood, state, or nation. They are approaches to serving the less fortunate that develop as monologues in which those in need are talked about and tended to by those who perceive themselves as need-less; that is, they are attempts to serve and save others, whether or not those others want to be served or are in need of saving. Each concept, in its own way, develops into practice that emphasizes the privilege and power inherent in oppressive relationships.

Service as punishment, a practice common in legal judgments in and out of public schools (and one increasingly manifested in prisoners "working" along public venues such as roads, highways, and interstates), is not only unworkable—it is dangerous to the practice of community service (and democracy itself) as it can develop into a powerful tool used to control already marginalized students and lends negativity to serving one's community. Even volunteerism, when closely examined, does not have the characteristics necessary to successfully implement a CSL project. What follows is a closer examination of each of these oppressive service concepts.

Philanthropy as Community Service

Robert Payton helps clarify the notion of philanthropy when he says, "one-way transfers are not all philanthropic, but all philanthropic transfers are one-way."[6] Payton argues that philanthropy has developed (especially so recently) as a means to help the needy in the face of a declining market interest in state-sponsored welfare.[7] Utilizing a market analysis, Peyton suggests that philanthropy is an economic endeavor that is a one-way transfer of means and is a desirable replacement for lost interest in state-sponsored, public financial support for the needy. Philanthropy, in this sense, is what Payton calls the "third sector" (the other two being the public and private sectors). Though Payton suggests that some form of dialogue between haves and have-nots is implied in the conception and practice of philanthropy, it is the dialogue of the market: if I help you, then you owe something to someone; if not now, then in the future.[8]

Brian O'Connell mirrors Payton's ideas in suggesting that philanthropy ought to "fill-in" where government support could not or should not do so. As such, he regards philanthropy as an important part of "personal and national freedom."[9] Similarly to Payton, O'Connell calls the endeavor a "discourse"; however, it is a discourse among the wealthy, not between the needy and those who provide for that need. Nor does philanthropy account at all for the possibility that the served can provide an educational service to the servers or that those providing the service are in need as well.[10]

As to my specific concern here—that of developing a reasonably sound philosophy of community service for CSL—philanthropy is simply inappropriate. The philanthropic discourse of the privileged and powerful simply giving money to those perceived as needy further complicates those lost connections evidenced in ever-growing socio-economic, racial, and political divisions. In fact, and as several critics argue, philanthropy, as most often practiced, is antithetical to a vibrant democracy.[11]

Nor is philanthropy educational in any meaningful way—certainly an issue to be considered in CSL. As the progressives argued, and as I will argue in a subsequent chapter, "to learn it, is to live it." In a philanthropic act there is no living it, no genuine social *interaction*—interaction (or transaction) that is necessary for active reconstruction of problematic experience. There is no opportunity to "feel with" the other, in the words of Nel Noddings, and therefore there is no opportunity to learn about the other.[12] Philanthropy ignores the powerful reconstructive learning process that is part of solving a felt problem and necessary to the educational process; as John Dewey, Paul Hanna, and William H. Kilpatrick argued, direct experience, mediation, planning, action, and evaluation to see what resultant change has occurred in the problematic situation are essential to learning.[13]

In short, philanthropy does not provide for a direct reconstruction of the needful situation or a reconstruction of self in regard to situations of need. Lacking meaningful interaction in experience, reflective thinking does not occur or it is incomplete, and learning to manipulate ideas in genuine experience does not happen. This lack leads future philanthropic experiences to be equally miseducative (or worse), and stagnation rather than growth results. Philanthropy clearly is not an understanding of service that can be relied on to direct CSL projects.

Charity as Community Service

Though there are subtle and important nuances among philanthropy and its sister concepts charity and noblesse oblige, the problems they bring to the implementation of CSL projects are nearly identical. Charity is more than simply a financial attack on the problems of society, such as that practiced by philanthropists. There is often direct personal service as well. Charity, however, is no more useful an idea than philanthropy when it comes to CSL projects. As Benjamin Barber points out, "the language of charity drives a wedge between self-interest and altruism, leading students to believe that service is a matter of sacrificing private interests to moral virtue."[14] This concept of service leads to one-way interactions where only a one-way transfer is seen as important.

As with philanthropy, charity portrays service as an endeavor in which only the served has needs and only the server has goods, and as Barber suggests, is not self-reconstructive in any way to the server beyond meeting some moral (often religious) expectations— service as a sign of being a good person who does "good works."

Robert Coles, in *The Call of Service*, writes that charity is "an old-fashioned name for much that gets called service.... For some of us the word has patronizing implications—toss 'them' something called 'charity.'"[15] His father understood this problem as well: he "was critical of comfortable people giving an hour or two here or there and utterly avoiding taking a hard look at how our institutions work (and for whom)."[16] Certainly, like philanthropy, charity can and does provide important stopgap means of support for Americans in temporary need. It is not helpful, however, in the implementation of CSL. There is nothing in the charity experience that is educational to the server; community division rather than community connection can be the result; and the service does not solve anything (as Paul Hanna suggested it should). Nor does an act of charity include the institutional critique necessary for broad social solutions to broad social problems. As Coles remembers,

> "We don't want your damn charity" was a refrain I heard from many poor people, black and white, in the South and in Appalachia; they were determined to claim as a right what others offered as a gesture of personal generosity.[17]

Benjamin Barber makes clearer the objection to the notion of service as a one-way transfer such as that found in the concepts of philanthropy and charity. He correctly argues that in a democracy it is the *interaction* of server and served that is most important to democratic community building, construction of self, and democratic education. Barber writes in *An Aristocracy of Everyone*:

> Many draw a misleading and dangerous picture of service as the rich helping the poor or the poor paying a debt to their country as if "community" means only the disadvantaged and needy and does not include those performing service.[18]

Viewing service in reverse, many participants in charity serve (give money and time) in order to assuage their guilt about being one of the haves rather than the have nots, thus debasing the monologue even further than what Barber suggests. The working out of economic guilt transforms charity into a completely self-serving activity.[19] In this case, as one well-known cultural critic has said:

> The guiding purpose here is the spiritual animation of the giver, not the alms he dispenses. The person who has given a year in behalf of someone or something else is himself better for the experience. National service is not about reducing poverty; it is about inducing gratitude.[20]

Clearly this is not a workable notion for CSL education.

Noble Obligation as Community Service

The idea of noblesse oblige is an even more un-democratic and miseducative concept than is charity. It denotes an aristocratic obligation. As such, it is part and parcel of the language and practice of European aristocracy, complete with noble breeding and the responsibilities that come with it. Rarely is noblesse oblige mentioned by name in discussions of community service because of its bald-faced reference to undemocratic and clearly oppressive practice. Unfortunately, it is often the most characteristic of many CSL programs. When it comes to the service component of CSL, active interaction between "server" and "served" is essential. Without discussions about why one has democratic obligations to others, and void of worthwhile reflection on what one who serves may receive in return from the service, service involvement degenerates into privileged obligation. The conceptual assumption of privilege perpetuates the belief that social-class division is natural to a democracy and that one's position in that system indicates individual worth.

Punishment as Community Service

Another practice that should be divorced from CSL is compulsory service as punishment. This practice is commonly found in public-school settings as well as at criminal sentencing hearings. Unfortunate ties between rule breaking and service have developed as community service is assigned more and more often as part of a criminal sentence, especially for youth. In many public schools, rule breakers can be found performing service to the school as punishment for unacceptable behavior. This service at schools often takes the form of custodial chores performed before, during, or after the school day. It's reminiscent of the chain-gang mentality (still in vogue in some states) that viewed service performed in public as proof that rule breakers will be punished. It's assigned with the hope that it will deter others from breaking rules.

The ramifications of associating community service with punishment are far reaching. As a form of punishment, service develops into a political tool that the powerful use to correct and control the behavior of the powerless. The results are particularly acute when the punishment takes place without reflection about why the behavior was unacceptable and how the service is related to the misdeed. Students, understandably, perceive service to be something that results from misbehavior, rather than as an educational experience, much less as a democratic obligation. When service is punishment, the "call to service" can be destroyed.

Volunteerism as Community Service

A concept regaining popularity recently, particularly as public schools look for parental and other adult involvement, is that of volunteerism. "Volunteer" has an altruistic ring to it. It means, simply, one who gives freely of oneself. However, upon examining the language and practice associated with volunteering, it becomes clear that the concept is only partially helpful in understanding the service in CSL. It is incomplete because, as Howard Radest argues, like philanthropy, charity, noblesse oblige, and punishment, volunteerism lacks an understanding of democratic community building and connecting:

> Community service also conveys a transcending purpose which volunteering does not. It endorses the search for the lost connection even while it is ambivalent about the virtues of those to whom it is addressed. The volunteer, although seldom alone in his or her task, responds as an individual. He or she is the autonomous citizen making a personal choice. In the appeal to volunteers we are directed to the work to be done. The community service participant, on the other hand, is embedded in an environment filled with symbols and references, a gender and class and caste environment, and finally a preparatory environment. Community service is addressed to the participant's needs as much as if not more than to the work to be done. It is addressed too, to the transcending purposes of the work to be done. In a sense, the present is more significant for the volunteer than the past or the future. But it is the past and the future which help to make sense of community service.[21]

The idea of volunteering lacks the essential democratic notion of communal connection that results from a freedom to understanding community, ignores the ramifications of history and its impact on the present/future and therefore must be avoided in CSL projects.

Mutuality as Community Service

The elimination of these traditionally oppressive notions of service for supporting CSL projects is helpful, but incomplete. There remains the project of constructing a comprehensive understanding of service that might most completely and reasonably support CSL. The most obvious shortcoming common to each of the above conceptions of service is that they ignore the essential dialectical nature of community service. Instead, each paints a picture of service as action with little or no substantial interaction (or, as Thayer-Bacon suggests, transaction). A concept commonly and successfully employed to explain the interaction that should occur in CSL projects is mutuality, or synonymously, reciprocity. Howard Radest, among others, argues that mutuality is one valuable conceptual component of sound community service.[22]

The concept of mutuality takes into account the fact that community service is based on the perception of need: "Need is a leading character in community service. Where I am in the story, however, shapes its meaning for me. With the encounter, the idea of need becomes problematic."[23] The problem that comes in the encounter with those in a perceived state of need is precisely that of oppression, as discussed above. With need come the needy and, more often than not, a power relationship. Admitting need is admitting, among other things, that class divisions exist; and listening to the needy often means admitting that the American Dream is nothing more than a myth perpetuated in support of social and economic reproduction. The admitting of class division in service distinguishes the server and the served and separates rather than connects the two groups of "strangers," particularly when service is conceived in any of the above oppressive ways.

For community service to work in CSL, these dividing lines must be blurred in the understanding that the server is also in need and receives a service as well as providing one—this blurring of lines is entailed in most understandings of mutuality. The needs that can be met on the part of the server (students and teachers particularly) include a richer conception of human diversity; a deeper understanding of the particular population being served; insights into social reproduction; a criticality of systemic oppression; and, seeing that academics are essential to solving lived difficulties. It is this intense interaction—described here as mutuality or reciprocity—that makes CSL socially and politically powerful, for it is through mutual interaction that the lessons of the served to the server can be learned and thereby influence future behavior, making the interaction an educative experience. It is also through the interaction of server and served that academic or technical skills can be enhanced through their ethical use. Mutuality explains that not only is academic/cognitive training expanded through the interactive, transactional service experience, but so is learning about unfamiliar social worlds and developing new ethical dispositions crucial to democratic connection. It is the interaction, or the "two-wayness," of the stranger-self relationship that is important and mandated by the idea of mutuality particularly in CSL projects.

Robert Rhoads points out that the idea of mutuality is echoed in numerous discussions of the community-service ethic.[24] For Jane Kendall, mutuality is "the exchange of both giving and receiving between the 'server' and the person or group 'being served'" and is the core concern of community service.[25] Nel Noddings, in advocating a moral ethic of care, suggests that the interaction between server and served should be seen not simply as empathy, but as a receiving of the other as part of him- or herself:

> The notion of "feeling with" that I have outlined does not involve projection but reception. I have called it "engrossment." I do not "put myself in the other's shoes," so to speak, by analyzing his reality as objective data and then asking, "How would I feel in such a situation?" On the contrary, I set aside my temptation to analyze and to plan. I do not project; I receive the other into myself, and I see and feel with the other. I become a duality. [26]

For Noddings, one becomes emotionally attached to the other in the reciprocity of the service act. In any of these ways of seeing service, it is the persistence of otherness that generates the mutual, interactive relationship between doer and done-to.

The reciprocal relationships advocated by Kendall, Noddings, and Radest, can eliminate, or dilute, the hegemony between haves and have-nots that exists prior to a community service experience.

These writers answer the criticism I leveled earlier against the oppressive concepts of charity, philanthropy, noblesse oblige, and volunteerism by deepening what it means to encounter a stranger through service. Within this more complete scheme of service, mutuality becomes the core concept to understanding the service component of CSL as a dialogue that blurs the line between doer and done-to (and hints at the critical nature that CSL can have, which I discuss later in the book). The essence of service called for in CSL is contained in mutuality, and mutuality clearly reflects the understanding of community I outlined previously.

Howard Radest's Complete Notion of Service

Most CSL theory begins and ends with the concept of mutuality. Howard Radest, on the other hand, presents additional ideas that fully explain what community service means, particularly in CSL. In Radest's argument, understanding the service act can be satisfactorily complete only with the inclusion of two additional concepts: solidarity and diversity. In adding solidarity and diversity to mutuality in the understanding of service, Radest suggests a three-component service structure that greatly expands its understanding—one that can explain and support the service idea and its practice in CSL.

Radest's Mutuality

For Radest, the core concept of mutuality is explained by the reciprocal nature of the interaction between doer and done to and the social relationship that it magnifies:

> Community service introduces us tangibly to the reciprocities of doer and done-to. On the positive side, community service is a particular way of learning my human "being" precisely because it is an encounter of strangers with whom I am nevertheless connected by the possibility of a reciprocal interchange of positions. I can be doer; I can be done-to. On the critical side, community service is a way of challenging those relationships that separate human beings into the near-permanent haves of power and near-permanent have-nots of powerlessness . . . community service is not a transference of what is mine, my surplus of wealth, power, energy, to another as in acts of charity or acts of leadership but rather a restoration of what is mine and what is yours as human beings which actual situations have subverted or even destroyed. To be a doer in the presence of the done to is to respond to the other in myself. Both of us are active; neither is passive.[27]

Radest is careful not to imply that the reciprocal relationship found in such a notion of service could eliminate differences, particularly cultural differences:

> Mutuality should not be confused with similarity. It is precisely because the other remains the other and because I remain myself that community service works out. Our needs will not echo each other and where I am in need some other is able to respond.[28]

This explanation of mutuality emphasizes, as most discussions of mutuality do, that the one providing service receives as much or more than the one being served. The intense interaction between the server and the other provides the opportunity to practice classroom lessons, to reflect critically on the meaning of difference, and to develop a way to reach an understanding of what that difference means to the server and to a community. Mutuality provides the opportunity to experience a felt problem in the Deweyan sense and do the reflective thinking that Dewey describes.[29] The particular learning theory and concept of reflection embraced in this idea of the complete act of service will be discussed fully in the chapters that follow. Suffice it to say here that it is in mutuality that a problem is dealt with, and it is in mutuality that real and complete learning therefore occurs. The exchange of ideas and experiences between server and served develops critical, reflective skills and enhances academic training. As Richard Kraft puts it:

> In this interactive, dialogical form of reflection, individuals can explore each other's opinions, thoughts, desires, and perspectives. Without this emphasis on dialogue between individuals, service learning again becomes one-sided, focusing on the isolated views and perceptions of the student without true understanding of each individual's perspective. Misunderstanding and missed opportunities for learning can occur in isolated reflection.[30]

Clearly, mutuality is an important concept to understanding community service in CSL.

Solidarity

However, conceiving community service as simply a matter of mutuality ignores an important educational aspect of community service and, therefore, creates roadblocks to a complete understanding of CSL. Mutuality itself provides no understanding of dispositional preparation for future encounters with strangers—in Deweyan terms, mutuality alone cannot be educative because it does not account for the internalizing of habits that lead to future, richer service experiences.[31] As Radest puts it, "mutuality, after all, neglects my relationship with the stranger whom I do not encounter, neglects the idea of my readiness for encounters."[32] To deal with this conceptual shortcoming, Radest borrows from Richard Rorty and suggests a notion of solidarity:[33]

> Solidarity is the name of my relationship to the stranger who remains unknown—only a person in an abstract sense—but who is, like me, a human being. Solidarity is then a preparation for the future and at the same time a grounding in the present.[34]

As solidarity, service becomes habit forming in the Jamesian sense, for as James says,

> Every smallest stroke of virtue or of vice leaves its never so little scar. Nothing we ever do is, in strict scientific literalness, wiped out. As we become permanent drunkards by so many separate drinks, so we become saints in the moral, and authorities and experts in the practical and scientific spheres, by so many separate acts and hours of work.[35]

In this way, Radast's concept of solidarity develops into a disposition toward democratic interaction and service. It is a readiness to act, to respond to the stranger. It answers Dewey's demand that projects, to be educative, dispose the individual to future such experiences.[36] Solidarity is the "acknowledgements of relationships I could have, and in particular, relationships of being needed and being in need," and these acknowledgements "become part of my awareness of myself."[37]

Richard Rorty puts it in the following way: Solidarity "is to be achieved not by inquiry but by imagination, the imaginative ability to see strange people as fellow sufferers."[38] Solidarity, to use the language of Nel Noddings' feminism, is the ability to "feel with" the stranger.[39] As such, solidarity means that community service prepares one for encounters that might not happen, but could happen. It develops in the student not simply emotional readiness, but a cognitive and imaginative readiness as well. As Radest notes, "above all, solidarity calls for a certain generosity of perception, the will to find the other unthreatening in his or her otherness and to acknowledge the legitimacy of the call of the other upon me."[40]

This readiness for future encounters entailed in this view of service can be achieved best through experiential *and* academic preparation that develops in the student an understanding of the stranger—an understanding that makes empathy available within in the interaction. That "feeling with," together with the service experience, gives life to the service and to future stranger interactions. Solidarity then is an essential educational concept within the larger idea of community service, and particularly so for CSL. It is an attitude to be developed through and for successful community service and includes cognitive learning related to various forms of the stranger. It is also the realization that the doer (me) is just as much a stranger as the done to (the other). Only through this sense of solidarity will mutuality, reciprocity, or a "feeling with" be achieved.[41]

Mutuality and solidarity make service more understandable. However, though mutuality and solidarity explain the educational issues related to the service component, they do not satisfy the important question of democratic obligation. This obligation (one that Tocqueville observed more than a century and a half ago) results not from an aristocratic privilege as in noblesse oblige, but from organizing American life around the ideology of democracy rather than around a common cultural history or a communitarian-like "horizon" of choice.[42] To place CSL in democracy is to show the great promise it has as both an educational *and* a democratic undertaking.

Diversity

Mutuality and solidarity are born out of the fundamental otherness that is found in American democracy. This otherness, essential to democratic practice, must be understood in relationship to CSL so that its practice will succeed. To explain this democratic notion, Radest introduces his third component of service, diversity. Radest describes diversity as a "basic form of democratic sociability" that can be found not only in distant strangers, but also in those who are familiar to us. [43] Diversity is the realization from day-to-day living and institutional practice that each of us is different from one another in numerous public and private ways. Otherness appears, strangely enough, even when reflecting upon the differences (I and me) within one's own psyche. Otherness is reflective of John Dewey's belief that every experience makes us a somewhat different person when entering future similar experiences.[44]

The diversity recognized in otherness is particularly important to American democracy where responsibility comes through choice and not by inherited roles of responsibility. Choice does not relinquish one's responsibility: democratic choice justifies—in fact, necessitates—service as a democratic, problem-solving, and educational practice. The absence of inherited roles of responsibility also magnifies diversity of choice as well as diversity of selves. This is what Tocqueville meant when describing American character and democratic connection in relation to service. The freedom brought by a national structure grounded in personal choice rather than tradition is both exciting and frightening. Diversity, however, is not simply a matter of race, class, or caste, and solving problems of diversity is not simply a matter of calling for tolerance, understanding, or appreciation. As Radest suggests,

> Once the possibility of otherness opens up in as radical a form as it has now taken—diversity run wild or the normalization of differing "lifestyles" and "life worlds"—then, in a sense, human need and human response acquire novel content more and more rapidly. Added to the usual concerns of need—the typical issues of having and not having that stir the reformer—the encounter with strangers moves onto new territory. Community service in meeting the conditions of diversity initiates us into the organized practice of otherness. Above all, like art and vocation, it denies the temptation to "remain at home."[45]

Radest explains that the otherness that is played out in diverse lifestyles, beliefs, and histories compels American citizens to serve others within a community; otherness demands that we not "stay at home"; otherness requires community-service solutions to local problems. Otherness, understood through the idea of diversity, is a vital part of any education that is democratic. CSL is no exception.

Diversity, in its recognition of the elusive character of the American individual, completes the notion of service fitting for CSL. It is the understanding that in any service situation there must exist a dialogue between server and served, and the line between the two groups is blurred in that dialogical interaction. Diversity requires that needs of both server and served are met by the other. Diversity necessitates democratic connection that can be achieved through CSL. Service, understood in this way, is educative in that it anticipates future encounters, and service thus envisioned teaches that diversity is the essential and unavoidable fact of the democratic experience. Service in CSL should seek to connect diverse populations, thereby allowing democratic practice to thrive, and in its strongest understanding, allow for a critique of systemic oppression. Service thus envisioned is grounded in a conception of community that is based on a freedom to understanding of liberty as laid out in Chapter Five—the understanding that individual freedom is dependent on a particular kind of relationship between individual and community—a relationship grounded in mutuality, solidarity, and diversity.

Community Service and the Mundane

Finally, Radest makes an important distinction between community service as a response to a crisis, and as normal, ordinary, mundane democratic habits of behavior. And though he indicates that conceiving community service as "ordinary" might be utopian, he argues that community service as a reaction to crisis makes it impossible to shift our metaphorical understandings of ourselves as wholly individual, to a democratically oriented understanding of association and support:

> Community service would appear differently if it was conceived under conditions of ordinariness. We would simply be "of service" to each other, be for each other and not require the inducement of danger. But, crisis itself has become ordinary in a world so given to inequalities, to gaps between what is and what is desirable, to failures of response, to blindness and deafness not only to others but to one's self. I am trying to avoid the delusions of crisis become routine. Yet, this routine is precisely what the bounded and momentary nature of community serve programs acknowledges. In a sense, the doer knows that he or she is doing something and yet, that really doing something—bridging the gulf between doer and done-to-is not on the agenda.[46]

Radest concludes that

> Community service introduces concreteness into a "conversation" that would otherwise deal in merely symbolic encounters. Indeed, without it we would, as it were, be looking at the travelogue but not doing the traveling, and for ethics and politics, this is a particularly serious indictment. At the same time, the appeal to practice is dangerous, particularly in an environment that invites us to be spectators, to operate "by

the numbers" and to pay for surrogates. We are easily misled into confusing doing with secondary activities like fundraising, going to meetings, signing petitions and the like.[47]

The service in CSL demands that teachers and students leave the classroom to encounter other living communities where strangers might become familiars. In this way, democratic education aids the establishment of new connections for a truly moral democracy in America.

Implications for Practice

What does this three-part service framework—mutuality, solidarity, and diversity—mean for CSL practice? First and foremost, and again following the thought of John Dewey, this framework demands that the service come about as a means to solve a truly felt problem. This conception of service assumes that the service is (to be colloquial) "for real." If the service conversation is not about a real problem, it is merely posturing and politicking. If there is no problem, there is no need to serve. If the problem has been invented or is neither felt by the served nor the servers, artificial or false understanding will result and hegemonic social relationships will remain. As John Dewey explains, "general appeals to a child to think, irrespective of the existence in his own experience of some difficulty that troubles him and disturbs his equilibrium, are as futile as advice to lift himself by his boot-straps."[48]

The requirement that need exists and is perceived puts the instructor in a place much different than that conceived for teachers traditionally. In fact, it clearly calls for P–12 teachers to be similar, if not precisely the same, as that suggested by John Dewey and the other progressive educators mentioned in Chapter Three.[49] It is the teacher's responsibility to lead her students close enough—physically, intellectually, and emotionally—to problematic situations that they feel them and are inclined to solve them. In this understanding of service and education, it is paramount that the teacher respects the interests and felt problems of her students. She must help construct situations that make her students sensitive to problems and their possible solutions, just as Paul Hanna suggested in his discussion of community service. Dewey says about this:

> The point that I have been wishing so far to make is that the possibility of having knowledge become something more than the mere accumulation of facts and laws, of becoming actually operative in character and conduct, is dependent on the extent to which that information is evolved out of some need in the child's own experience and to which receives application to that experience.[50]

The CSL instructor must view education not as preparation *for* life, but *as* life complete with problems to be solved and experiences to be remade. She then must provide ways of solving problems through action both in and out of the classroom. In this way, the service activity leads to learning that becomes "operative in character and conduct."

Mutuality demands a particularly intense approach to solving the felt problem. It requires an interaction, a transaction, a conversation. Mutuality demands that students meet with strangers such that hegemony be eliminated or at least blurred. Mutuality calls for an interaction that goes beyond the surface realization that a problem exists and beyond the mere volunteerism discussed earlier. When Nel Noddings suggests that in caring and serving one must feel with another, she means much more than a simple realization and temporary fix of a problem.[51] The interaction called for in the notion of mutuality is one that can come only with intense and regular encounters with strangers in need. For P–12 schools operating under the CSL educational philosophy, it means providing face-to-face encounters between students and strangers.

The reciprocal interaction called for in mutuality will be educative beyond what any classroom alone can provide. These regular encounters can soften and ultimately eliminate the power relationship that exists between student and stranger (and, of course, the students may also be the "stranger-in-need").Ultimately, the stranger no longer will be the stranger; instead, community connection and a feeling with will replace the stranger relationship. The realization of need will replace the desire for power.

Though the interaction called for by mutuality is essential to the service endeavor in CSL, classroom activity cannot be ignored. With Radest's foundational concept of solidarity comes the preparatory matter that is necessary in the classroom prior to and following an encounter with the stranger. This educational preparation is aside from any academic understanding gained through the service activities themselves. Solidarity requires that students entering into a service encounter be prepared so that a "generosity of perception" and a "will to find the other unthreatening" are developed in the students.[52] It is in the solidarity idea that habit formation is taken into account through prior preparation. If students are to serve successfully, they must have some understanding of the strangers they encounter. If they are to truly learn, they must, as John Dewey argued, be provided experiences that will open future experiences.[53]

For example, if students are serving a nursing-home population, before the service is performed, the students must be prepared for and explore what to expect of nursing-home patients and the elderly generally. This continuing preparation (it cannot end when service begins) might take the form of reading fiction, nonfiction, viewing films, and other texts accompanied by discussions to prepare the students for the initial service encounter.[54] These classroom activities must continue throughout the service and bring an increasing depth of understanding, as the stranger becomes the familiar. Academic preparation not only undergirds the ensuing particular service activity, but also will advance solidarity generally for future encounters with strangers. The preparation will develop the habit of readiness to interact open-mindedly with other similar strangers for which solidarity calls. It is also necessary that some debriefing, or reflection, occur following the service. Reflection (which will be fully discussed in Chapter Eight) is essential to developing that sense of solidarity called for by Radest. Finally, service conceived of and practiced in this way will provide the opportunity to put classroom theory to use, thereby entrenching academic learning and its value as an essential problem-solving tool.

The readiness for specific encounters, and the general habit of readiness for future encounters with strangers within this three-component conception of service, brings students to the important realization of "persistent otherness," or diversity. This is particularly important for making community connections in a democracy, as well for examining systemic oppression. Diversity is the realization that we have an ethical responsibility to connect with each other through community service and thereby know the diverse and numerous others that make up a community in a moral democracy—a system based on creed rather than history or ethnicity.

Diversity also reminds teachers and students alike that every individual is a stranger in one way or another, and every individual is in need. Without the notion of diversity, the realization that we all participate as strangers in some way or other is lost. Without correctly understanding diversity, democratic connection and the sense of time and place called for in CSL will not develop. Without that understanding, service degenerates into volunteerism where act rather than connection is the focus. For the CSL practitioner, it's important to make sure that throughout the process there are opportunities to encounter diversity, and to emphasize differences while simultaneously celebrating commonality: "We're all in this together." We are diverse—and communal. Such regular encounters will develop a deeper understanding of difference, one that reaches far beyond simply being tolerant or appreciative.

Conceptualizing service in the manner described here makes CSL an important part of democratic education. Mutuality, solidarity, and diversity, when practiced correctly in CSL, can provide students with opportunities to learn essential democratic notions. CSL also gives students the opportunity to develop a deep sense of self and a deep understanding of the other. Alexis de Tocqueville explained nearly a century and a half ago that it is precisely these characteristics that a democracy needs to prevent the despotism that he feared would destroy it. CSL is, therefore, an approach to education that is demanded by our political system and is the responsibility of America's system of public and private education. Only through an education that is part of, not apart from, the community, and that serves through interacting with the community, can democratic principles be taught and learned in a way that is supportive of the grown-up liberalism I suggested earlier.

Many recent studies have shown that participation in basic democratic institutions, such as the practice of voting, has been seriously declining over the last several decades.[55] Robert Putnam and others view this decline as a sign that connections once established through community activity are increasingly being broken and lost. Putnam, Robert Bellah, and C. David Lisman see this disconnection as dangerous to democracy.[56] Participation in community activities provided by CSL, when service is correctly understood and practiced, can go a long way in re-establishing these disintegrating connections—connections vital to community as described in the previous chapter.

As Howard Radest, Nel Noddings, Robert Bellah, Robert Rhoads and Jane Kendall argue, reconnection is an essential, definitive goal of community service.[57] CSL education is a public practice that can redefine connection and defend against the individualism that Tocqueville argued would leave its citizens prey to tyranny. CSL, when its service component is understood and practiced as described here, is a way to defend American democracy against the growing practices that divide rather than connect, and keep Americans from the increasing selfish individualism characterized in our growing habit of "bowling alone."

In the community-service act, it is hoped that students learn; that depends on a clear epistemological perspective. I will now turn to a discussion of experiential education.

CHAPTER SEVEN

Epistemology

Introduction

CSL's epistemological component is universally understood to be "experiential," and I certainly agree.[1] On the other hand, universal agreement in name does not necessarily entail a universality, or depth, of understanding. To the contrary, simply calling CSL "experiential" and having everyone nod in agreement carries with it the danger of oversimplification—as demonstrated when experiential epistemology is variously described as "hands-on" (unfortunately so), "minds-on" (whatever that means), "learning by doing," and so forth. The truth is that experiential pedagogies are both simpler and simultaneously more complicated than traditional, typically teacher-centered educational practices. They are simpler in that they mirror lived experience; and more complicated in their actual implementation. They are also completely dependent upon having developed a sound theory of human experience, which is certainly a complicated endeavor.[2] Those complications are magnified when experiential theory is tied to notions of community, service, reflection, and democracy as is the case with CSL.

When you add to these purely theoretical complications the fact that CSL is only one methodological manifestation of experiential learning theory among many, that there has been an explosive growth of literature devoted to experiential educational practice over the last 40 years, and that all pedagogical approaches are ultimately experiential (even the half-dozing lecture participant "experiences" the lecture), it's easy to see how and why the conceptual epistemological waters of CSL (and therefore, its means) have become muddied.[3] My aim with this chapter is to address the complications noted above by revisiting the experiential theory initially constructed by those pragmatic philosophers discussed in Chapter Three, with particular attention to how that theory fits within the conceptions of community and service.

Traditional Notions of Learning and Knowledge

In explaining his rebellion from traditional educational notions, John Dewey pointed out that "the history of educational theory is marked by opposition between the idea that education is development from within and that it is formation from without." [4] Throughout its history, epistemological theory has had a parallel pendulum swing between Platonic idealism and Lockean empiricism.[5] These pendulum swings characterize the either-or history (as Dewey described it) of epistemological /learning theory.[6]

Dewey saw that three characteristics fundamentally drove traditional educational philosophy and practice: (1) already established bodies of information and skills are seen as being "transmitted" to students; (2) habits of conduct are developed through conformity to pre-established standards and rules; and (3) schools, as institutions, are "marked off from" other community institutions (hence the importance of a community theory to educational practice generally, and CSL particularly).[7] Dewey clarified both the aims and means of traditional education from these three general characteristics:

> The main purpose or objective is to prepare the young for future responsibilities and for success in life, by means of acquisition of the organized bodies of information and prepared forms of skill which comprehend the material of instruction. Since the subject-matter as well as standards of proper conduct are handed down from the past, the attitude of pupils must, upon the whole, be one of docility, receptivity, and obedience. Books, especially textbooks, are the chief representatives of the lore and wisdom of the past, while teachers are the organs through which pupils are brought into effective connection with the material. Teachers are the agents through which knowledge and skill are communicated and rules of conduct enforced.[8]

Jeffrey Howard says it this way: "In the traditional teaching-learning model, learning is individualistic and privatized; students generally learn by themselves and for themselves. The epistemology that under girds traditional pedagogy is positivistic and in conflict with communal ways of learning."[9] In light of the communal nature of service and the community theory outlined in Chapter Five, the traditional, teacher-centered, individualistic, competitive educational model that Dewey and Howard critique is not simply inconsistent with CSL; it is antithetical to CSL.

The Progressive Epistemological Revolution and CSL

The "either-orness" against which Dewey and his cohorts fought early in the 20th century was founded on a widely accepted epistemological dualism that kept mind and matter separated, emphasizing education from within, or education from without, rather than the interaction/transaction of subject with her object of study. For the progressives, and informed by the philosophy of pragmatism, it was simply nonsensical to talk of subject and object as separate and separated entities. Human experience (and by implication, experiential education), the progressives argued, is grounded in an inherent interaction of subject with object, not in imagining the two existing in separate ontological categories of knowing. The traditional dualistic epistemology was the basis for developing educational practices (described metaphorically by Paulo Freire as the "banking system"[10]) wherein teaching is nothing more than the transmission of already established forms of knowledge to a passive learner. Progressive epistemology, on the other hand, suggested that learning happens via active experiential reconstruction that results in new ways of knowing and doing. Subject/object interaction, rather than ontological separation of the knower and the known, is the basis for experiential education generally, and CSL specifically; and, it is interaction/transaction that makes CSL the reconnecting, communal, critical, and therefore educational practice it can and should be.

Bacon's Science, Kant's Critique, and James' Radical Empiricism

As John Dewey argued, Francis Bacon came to understand science and philosophy as dynamic projects involving the interaction of subject and object rather than merely the study of static concepts. Bacon's insight undermined traditional epistemological theory and ultimately led to a different and pragmatically better understanding of the purposes and methods of inquiry, knowledge construction, and by implication, educational practice.[11] Bacon saw that the goal of scientific inquiry is to control nature rather than to control minds, and that could be achieved only by conceptualizing scientific discovery as an interaction of mind and matter in experience.

Similarly, in his attempt to account for empirical philosophy (understood briefly as the idea that the human mind can *only* "know" via experience), particularly that of David Hume, Immanuel Kant suggested that the human mind orders experience with reference to space and time—both being forms, importantly, of human perceiving and as such predisposing us to knowing the world in particular ways.[12] As expressed in his critical philosophy (or transcendental imagination in the first edition of *Critique of Pure Reason*), Kant takes account of the knower in relationship to the known—a uniting of subject and object. This philosophical treatment of perception and knowledge are reflective of Bacon's science and precursors to both James' radical empiricism and Dewey's revolutionary experiential epistemology.

Because knowledge is created through this foundational mind/matter interaction, educational practice should be founded on that interaction as well. CSL is, of course, no exception: the subject/object, student/situation transaction on which CSL projects (should) focus makes CSL educationally powerful. Through manipulating or reconstructing the project problem, academic knowledge, self-understanding, and broad institutional insights can be constructed—self and world can be transformed.

William James' understanding of interactive experience, radical empiricism, provides further foundational grounding for CSL. He saw, as did Bacon and Kant, that it is within experiential interaction, not without, that humans construct knowledge, hone skills, and critically transform both self and the things of the world:

> He [the pragmatist] turns away from abstraction and insufficiency, from verbal solutions, from bad a priori reasons, from fixed principles, closed systems, and pretended absolutes and origins. He turns towards concreteness and adequacy, towards facts, towards action and towards power. That means the empiricist temper regnant and the rationalist temper sincerely given up. It means the open air and possibilities of nature, as against dogma, artificiality, and the pretence of finality in truth.[13]

James' understanding of the pragmatic construction of knowledge, the understanding that knowing is not a problem of mind somehow grasping alien substance, but is one of mind and body interacting with substance, implies, essentially, that an activitysuch as CSL can be educationally and communally transformative only when the activity is one deeply imbued with interaction of self and matter, and selves with other selves (a reflection of community as conceived of earlier). CSL projects, as a purely academic matter, must be fundamentally based on this understanding of experiential interaction.

In an article characterizing the influence that James has had on experiential educational theory, George Donaldson and Richard Vinson tease out of his "Lectures to Teachers and Students," eleven basic principles of experiential education.[14] These eleven principles echo much of what I've previously suggested are the hallmarks of CSL projects:

> 1. One learns best by his/her own activity. 2. Interest is of signal importance to learning. 3. Sensory experience is basic. 4. Effort and vigor make for good education. 5. Education modifies behavior. 6. Good education is holistic. 7. Imitating exemplary behavior is sound learning. 8. Love and understanding are important to learning. 9. Effective learning is interdisciplinary. 10. Respect for individual differences is essential. 11. Sound education is specific.[15]

Donaldson and Vinson argue that William James was the "philosophical father" of experiential education. He was the first to extend his pragmatism to education so directly, and it was out of his thinking that progressive scholars developed a fully fleshed-out educational theory based on experience—one that fundamentally supports CSL.

John Dewey's Revolutionary Epistemology

Arguing that CSL should be viewed as an attempt to "dePlatonize" western educational thought, Ira Harkavy and Lee Benson note that "it can fairly be said: in the beginning there was Dewey."[16] Very little of the literature on CSL's epistemology (including this book) is absent references to the revolutionary work of John Dewey. In what follows, I hope to connect Dewey's pragmatic learning theory more directly to CSL given that it points to important practical implications for CSL implementation.[17]

Dewey grounded his argument for an experiential notion of education in an explicit assumption that had been missed in the traditional ways and means of educational practice. That fundamental assumption is that "there is an intimate and necessary relationship between the processes of actual experience and education."[18] It is a simple and straightforward assumption. However, current educational practice based on traditional epistemology largely ignores the intimacy between experience and education.

Traditional teaching generally dismisses experience out of hand.
As Richard Hopkins maintains

> The secondary schools in particular show in their instructional practices
> an almost total disregard for the experience of students. They are arenas
> of intense control and manipulation endured by an objectified, disembo-
> died, and often alienated student population. For many students, even
> those who have learned how to work the system, attending school is an
> inauthentic experience to be endured until real life begins.[19]

Artificial curriculum constraints (a growing constraint in contemporary educational policy), student preparation for life in some
adult future, and the consideration of student experience as secondary to the digestion and regurgitation of pre-established facts
are all antithetical to CSL. It is crucial that CSL educators first
and foremost understand the "intimate and necessary" relationship between experience and education and incorporate that into
practice. The experience/education relationship can best be understood as interactive, social, and continual.

Because education is experiential, it is interactive at a very basic, existential level. That is, human beings are born into a world
of objects, and it is by interacting and manipulating the physical
world that humans come upon and solve basic problems of existence. Dewey explained in *Democracy and Education* that

> As long as it [a living creature] endures, it struggles to use surrounding
> energies in its own behalf. It uses light, air, moisture, and the material of
> soil. To say that it uses them is to say that it turns them into means of
> its own conservation. As long as it is growing, the energy it expends in
> thus turning the environment to account is more than compensated for
> by the return it gets: it grows. Understanding the word "control" in this
> sense, it may be said that a living being is one that subjugates and con-
> trols for its own continued activity the energies that would otherwise use
> it up. Life is a self-renewing process through action upon the environ-
> ment.[20]

On its face, this observation appears to have little to do with CSL
and seems so strongly a truism as to not need comment. However,
further analysis shows that understanding experience in this way
is a crucial building block to successful CSL practice.

The importance of the physical fact of existence to CSL is that
the experience of manipulating objects is essential to learning and
living. It is pedagogically imperative that young people develop

skills and dispositions through genuine object manipulation, because it is the most essential interactive life activity. Without it, knowledge cannot be constructed, nor life problems solved. The increasing complexity of that manipulation leads to further success with physical objects and ultimately to the manipulation of ideas to solve problems in experience. For CSL to be successful as an educational approach, students must manipulate physical objects and mental constructs in the project situation, interacting with both the people and the things of the world. Manipulating the physical and mental environment in a service project provides students with the opportunity to use their knowledge of the world to attempt a solution to the service problem. It is out of this basic understanding of interaction that the increasingly complex academic disciplines of mathematics, chemistry, and physics, for example, can be taught, applied and therefore learned in CSL.

Human interaction, of course, does not involve individuals interacting only with objects and ideas. Humans are not born into a purely objective reality, but arrive in a world that has an already established social organization with already existing social beings. Education is the means by which individuals are introduced into social practice. Education, argues Dewey, is essentially a social process, and the social component of learning is often ignored in traditional epistemological approaches:

> There is the standing danger that the material of formal instruction will be merely the subject matter of the schools, isolated from the subject matter of life-experience. The permanent social interests are likely to be lost from view. Those which have not been carried over into the structure of social life, but which remain largely matters of technical information expressed in symbols, are made conspicuous in schools. Thus we reach the ordinary notion of education: the notion which ignores its social necessity and its identity with all human association that affects conscious life, and which identifies it with imparting information about remote matters and the conveying of learning through verbal signs: the acquisition of literacy.[21]

A sound educational approach, on the other hand, takes into account the social-ness of human existence and incorporates that understanding into practice. It is, as Dewey argues, the social environment as it is constructed in experience that dictates the learning of social dispositions and habits of behavior. He argued in *Democracy and Education* that

The required beliefs cannot be hammered in; the needed attitudes cannot be plastered on. But the particular medium in which an individual exists leads him to see and feel one thing rather than another; it leads him to have certain plans in order that he may act successfully with others; it strengthens some beliefs and weakens others as a condition of winning the approval of others. Thus it gradually produces in him a certain system of behavior, a certain disposition of action.[22]

In this way, habits, or dispositions to act, are inculcated into the young.

It is vitally important that CSL practitioners understand and consciously incorporate this social aspect of learning into a service project; this social interaction is the basis for community, as conceptualized earlier, and is the source for self-development. As such, service projects are, as is argued in the previous chapter, examples of social interaction—an attempt at (re)connection. Mutuality, as it is ascribed to here, is the concept of give-and-take interaction between others. A successful CSL project incorporates the social idea of otherness. If a service project is constructed and carried out without keeping the social in mind, unintended habits or dispositions might well develop in place of desired ones, creating a miseducative experience.[23] As John Dewey implies, both academic (object/idea manipulation) and social (habit formation) aspects of a CSL project must be understood clearly if the educational goals of skill acquisition and habit formation are to be met. His notions of social and objective interaction might best be summarized in the following passage from *Experience and Education*:

It means, once more, that interaction is going on between an individual and objects and other persons. The conceptions of *situation* and of *interaction* are inseparable from each other. An experience is always what it is because of a transaction taking place between an individual and what, at the time, constitutes his environment, whether the latter consists of persons with whom he is talking about some topic or event, the subject talked about being also a part of the situation; or the toys with which he is playing; the book he is reading (in which his environing conditions at the time may be England or ancient Greece or an imaginary region); or the materials of an experiment he is performing. The environment, in other words, is whatever conditions interact with personal needs, desires, purposes, and capacities to create the experience which is had.[24]

The third Deweyan notion that is helpful for understanding CSL practice is his idea that experience implies continual growth.

He correctly points out that experience is a continuum; that is, present experience is grounded in the past and will modify the future.[25] An individual, therefore, is prepared for future life problems based on those that she has dealt with in the past. It is the effect of a present experience on future experiences that in part indicates the quality of that present experience, particularly educationally. When CSL projects are understood in this light, they become important not only to the task at hand, but are crucial building blocks for future problems that students will experience. Understanding experience as a continuum will also help to indicate what projects will and will not be educationally sound. With the idea of continuity in mind, projects can be developed that will provide the environment necessary for forming good habits of mind—academic and social. CSL projects, as I suggested earlier, have to be structured with future situations in mind (solidarity in service). To be successful, the projects must come out of genuine present problems of experience, while simultaneously looking to the future.

These notions of experience provide CSL educators with a foundation upon which to build successful projects. Truly educative CSL projects provide students the opportunity to operate in a genuine problem situation. The service project allows for the manipulation of objects and ideas related to academic endeavors, thereby creating a depth of understanding unmatched by traditional approaches. The project must be, to some degree, communal, for it is only through interacting with others that sought-after habits and dispositions can be developed in young people and true community transformation can be accomplished. Finally, CSL experiences should be chosen and organized such that students become open and eager for increasingly sophisticated projects of similar and different types: to be "educative" in the Deweyan sense, the most transformational CSL projects encourage the pursuit of future such experiences rather than stagnate, dull, or discourage such future pursuits. CSL projects done well, foment experiential growth.[26]

Further Progressive Support for Experiential Education in CSL

John Dewey was not alone in suggesting that education is inextricably connected to experience. William H. Kilpatrick and Paul

Hanna, in different ways, both advocated such CSL-like pedagogies. Kilpatrick suggested a project method approach to education driven by what he called a "purposeful act." For Kilpatrick, absent a purpose for an educational activity, a purpose deemed important by the individual student, that activity is useless. An educational activity that is not important in the eyes of the student leads to short-term rote performance rather than to the depth of understanding expected in CSL. The reader might recall the precipitating story of this book, remembering who decided on the PARKnership projects—it was not the students, which was probably the core reason for its lost potential.

Kilpatrick's idea of the purposeful act mirrors Dewey's essential suggestion that for an activity to be educative, it must be organized around the genuine interests of the student.[27] Kilpatrick writes,

> As these questionings rose more definitely to mind, there came increasingly a belief-corroborated on many sides—that the unifying idea I sought was to be found in the conception of wholehearted purposeful activity proceeding in a social environment, or more briefly, in the unity element of such activity, the hearty purposeful act.[28]

He provided a familiar example of how a purposeful act or lack thereof can make or break an educational project:

> If she did in hearty fashion purpose to make the dress, if she planned it, if she made it herself, then I should say the instance is that of a typical project. We have in it a wholehearted purposeful act carried on amid social surroundings. That the dressmaking was purposeful is clear; and the purpose once formed dominated each succeeding step in the process and gave unity to the whole [with apologies for the sexist assumptions].[29]

Kilpatrick adds an important component to CSL project choice and implementation. For a project to succeed educationally, it must originate in the interests and needs of the students—as Dewey would suggest, from an authentic felt problem. On further analysis, it becomes clear why this is so. Left to traditional notions of learning, educators tell students what projects are worthy of their attention (again, my PARKnership story) thereby ignoring the "powers and purposes of those taught."[30] The project becomes contrived and artificial because it disregards the personal needs, desires, purposes, and capacities of those who will be tackling the problem in the CSL situation. In a word, it lacks the unity of purpose called for by Kilpatrick. Not only must a CSL project be interactive, social, and continual; it must be driven by a purpose important to the students themselves.

Paul Hanna's contribution to CSL theory comes from the community side of the service equation and is reflective of the community notion laid out in Chapter Five. As I previously described, in 1936 the PEA commissioned a survey study entitled *Youth Serves the Community*. This study reported on myriad youth service projects from around the country. As Hanna found, educational service projects (as advocated by Kilpatrick) necessarily change the surrounding community: the community is remade in important ways. For Hanna, the "significant social value criteria" was as important as the "individual education criteria." I think it's important to the present context to repeat what Hanna suggested are the characteristics of a successful service project, and by extension, a successful CSL project in terms of community transformation:

> 1. Any project must culminate in the actual improvement of living in the community. 2. Projects must clearly be an obligation of youth as well as adulthood. 3. In so far as possible, projects must get at the basic problems of improving social welfare.[31]

As Hanna maintained, if schools are to be an integral part of the community, not marked off from it, they have certain obligations to their communities, and vice-versa. When developed without this understanding, CSL projects quickly become artificial and antithetical to experiential epistemology. CSL project interaction of individual and community is done with the goals of remaking the individuals involved *and* remaking the community. Only in that community reconstruction does the project becomes authentic, interactive, reconnecting, and educationally sound practice, which is called for by democratic community education that is inherently experiential.

The Experiential Learning Theory of David Kolb

Progressive educators such as James, Dewey, Kilpatrick, and Hanna provide a solid foundation upon which to base a variety of experiential educational approaches; and as is noted above, these thinkers are often (and correctly) relied upon to ground CSL practice. Many CSL advocates, however, have turned to other more contemporary thinkers to guide CSL educational activities. Of particular importance is the work of David Kolb. Kolb develops a brand of Deweyan progressivism in his widely read work *Experiential Learning*, from which many contemporary CSL models come.[32] Kolb contributes positively to experiential theory; on the other hand, there is an aspect of his notion of experiential learning that brings back an old problem—"either-orness."

In his introduction to *Experiential Learning*, Kolb credits Dewey as "the most influential educational theorist of the twentieth century, that best articulates the guiding principles for programs of experiential learning."[33] His book is, to a great extent, a reprise of Dewey's thought. In summarizing his position as it relates to Dewey, Kolb defines learning as "the process whereby knowledge is created through the transformation of experience."[34] He explains that this

> definition emphasizes several critical aspects of the learning process as viewed from the experiential perspective. First is the emphasis on the process of adaptation and learning as opposed to content or outcomes. Second is that knowledge is a transformation process, being continuously created and recreated, not an independent entity to be acquired or transmitted. Third, learning transforms experience in both its objective and subjective forms. Finally, to understand learning, we must understand the nature of knowledge, and vice versa.[35]

This, in summary form, is the position ascribed to in this study and comes directly from the work of John Dewey. In so far as Kolb revisits and re-examines the work of Dewey, and adds a contemporary readability to its substance, his work is an important addition to experiential learning theory.

However, Kolb expands upon the foundational work of earlier progressive philosophers and develops a model that takes into account contemporary research on learning styles and brain function. In particular, Kolb combines Dewey's experiential philosophy with learning style differences indicated by current work on right/left brain functioning. In this expansion of existing theory, Kolb introduces a different way of describing the thinking process that emphasizes learning styles associated with either right- or left-brain dominance.[36] He argues that adding contemporary brain research to experiential learning theory makes that theory stronger for driving educational practice.

At first glance, the addition of contemporary brain research to progressive theory is a positive development. It is crucial to incorporate new science into established theory. However, upon further analysis, Kolb's re-writing of experiential theory in light of new findings brings with it an old problem: it re-establishes a dualism in epistemological/learning theory. He invites teachers to view leaning as an "either-orness" of thinking *or* feeling, concrete experience *or* abstract conceptualization, and active experimentation *or* reflective observation, rather than as the integrated process that Dewey explicated in *How We Think*.[37] Kolb describes thinking as

> the making use of two dialectically opposed adaptive orientations...representing two different and opposed processes of grasping or taking hold of experience in the world—either through reliance on conceptual interpretation and symbolic representation, or through reliance on the tangible, felt qualities of immediate experience.[38]

Dewey, on the other hand, describes thinking and learning as a "train or chain" in which each successive step is associated intimately with previous and future steps—a complicated, often meandering process of emotional, mental, and physical movement coming out of living experienced problems and ultimately returning to experience with active solutions.[39] Kolb, in his discussion, limits the understanding of that process. He describes the experiential learning process as including only specific either/or ways of subject/object interaction. This rendering of experiential learning theory brings naïve simplicity to understanding the thinking (and, therefore, the learning) process—a simplicity that divides the thinking process and develops dualisms similar to those found in traditional epistemological theory. The consequence of Kolb's expansion of progressive thought is a return to understanding thinking and learning as an either-or project. Practice based on this extension of progressive thought has the danger of dividing rather than reconnecting those involved, as learners are grouped according to Kolb's "dialectically opposed" ways of knowing and modes of subject/object interaction are compartmentalized and divided—it is reductionist in its perspective rather than expansive.

In addition to my own reductionist critique, critical theorists such as David Thornton Moore argue that Kolb's theory suffers the same problem that I mentioned in Chapter Five: the over-reliance on the positivistic, objective, scientism that Thayer-Bacon finds troublesome. Moore writes of Kolb's theory:

> The post-structuralist will see that confrontation [between "shifting systems of meaning"] as more than an individual's struggle to compare ideas. Rather, as Foucault would argue, it must be seen as embedded in the histories of the respective institutions, and in the power arrangements underlying the definition and use of terms. So the learning process engages the student as a participant (generally with relatively little power) in an ongoing negotiation of meanings and their uses.[40]

Moore's sentiments also reflect the concerns of critical theorists mentioned earlier who see such reductionist, positivistic thinking as that of Kolb not accounting for the internalizing of repressive ideologies of the generalized other—an internalizing that occurs when learning is conceived as "a particular type of learner encountering a more or less given environment" rather than learning as "dialectical, emergent, situated and political."[41] Unfortunately, and Moore seems to agree with me on this, Kolb's view of experiential education is relied upon far too often in CSL theory and can restrict its successful practice as a reconnecting, reconstructive, communally/individually transforming democratic educational practice.

Implications for Practice

The experiential position outlined in this chapter has several important practical implications for CSL practice. First and foremost (and as I suggested in the previous chapter), a CSL teacher must conduct herself much differently than one in a traditional classroom practicing from a traditional epistemological position. The CSL teacher is an experiential guide for her students, not simply a "banker" providing already formulated knowledge to a passive student. As such, she has to have an understanding of the capacities, interests, and learning styles of her students while guiding them through and to problems that are sourced in their individual and social experiences. If, as Kilpatrick and Dewey have argued, the experience is not purposeful in character, it will be artificial, inauthentic and, therefore miseducative.

Second, project authenticity (a real, experienced problem) as required in CSL theory means that a CSL teacher has to understand the intimate and necessary relationship between experience and education as described by John Dewey. Individual, private, competitive notions of learning found in traditional classrooms do not take into account either the social or objective interaction called for by experiential learning theory. A CSL project must provide students with the opportunity to work with fellow students and strangers while manipulating the objects that are part of the project problem. Only in this kind of subject and object manipulation can social disposition (found in the concepts of diversity, mutuality, and solidarity), academic knowledge and skill, and communal understanding grow with the student. CSL practitioners/projects seek to educate the whole person—emotional stability, social sensibility, communal associability, physical sustainability, and academic ability—through authentic projects solving authentic problems. It is through just this type of social and object interaction that community problems are solved, knowledge is constructed, and ultimately, selves are recreated.

A third implication of viewing CSL as experiential is the integration of school and community. The interaction of community strangers in CSL projects provides opportunities to both educate *and* solve community problems. CSL projects can and should connect the school to the broader community. In this way, schools can avoid being marked off from other community institutions and be a vital part of democratic life. Paul Hanna makes clear that community impact must be an essential consideration for CSL projects. Lacking that communal impact, projects become inauthentic and are not characteristic of experiential learning as outlined here. This demand entails the grooming of relationships among school administrators, teachers, and community leaders that do not normally exist in traditional school settings.

Finally, and as John Dewey argued, experience should be seen as both the aim and means of education. As such, CSL projects should be designed with future experiences in mind. CSL teachers must guide projects so that students are open to future problem-solving activities. Growth is a process directed to the future. Educational growth means successfully moving onto more difficult problems/projects. Projects, therefore, should match the ability and maturity levels of the students involved. If they are not designed with this in mind, future CSL projects may be restricted rather than expanded.

The CSL P–12 teacher has a difficult task, which is much more demanding than what's called for in traditional notions of teaching, and is much more rewarding as well. The CSL educator must step outside traditional notions to an understanding that good education is an experiential process and that good teaching means guiding students through those problematic experiences important to them now. The service concept, when viewed as it is in Chapter Six of this study and combined with a view of education as experiential in nature, is an incredibly powerful pedagogy capable of reconnecting democratic citizens while educating them for successful democratic problem solving. Understanding community, service, and experiential learning are important steps to successful practice. However, these three are held together by a third component necessary for CSL education: reflective thinking. Community, service, and learning will remain disconnected and therefore incomplete without a full understanding of reflection in educational practice. Reflective thinking is the tie that binds community service to experiential learning, and it is to reflective thinking that I now turn.

CHAPTER EIGHT

Reflection: Binding Together Community, Service, and Learning

Introduction

In an article advocating the use of reflection maps in CSL, Janet Eyler argues:

> Reflection is the hyphen in service-learning; it is the process that helps students connect what they observe and experience in the community with their academic study. In a reflective service-learning class, students are engaged in worthwhile activity in the community, observe, make sense of their observations, ask new questions, relate what they are observing to what they are studying in class, form theories and plans of action, and try out their ideas.[1]

CSL advocates have long understood that reflection is the component that connects community-service activity with academics.[2] This interaction of community, service, and learning provides students with the opportunity to construct knowledge, meet strangers, solve communally felt problems and in so doing, reconstruct themselves; however, without the connection provided by reflection, community, service, and learning remain separate and therefore weak concepts for driving educational practice. Eyler writes, "In practice it is critical reflection . . .that provides the transformative link between the action of serving and the ideas and understanding of learning."[3] It is only through the correct understanding of reflection and its relationship to community, service, and academics that CSL projects can be educational at all.

Unfortunately, as has been long recognized, reflection is commonly the weakest component of a CSL project.[4] Eyler notes that the

most important component of a high-quality program is frequent attention to the reflective process. And while service itself has a positive effect
on personal development, if the objectives of service-learning include
such cognitive goals as deeper understanding of subject matter, critical
thinking, and perspective transformation, intensive and continuous reflection is necessary; little change is produced by classes that have community service as an add-on poorly integrated into the course.
Unfortunately, minimal or sporadic attempts to integrate service into the
course are fairly typical of service-learning classes.[5]

Eyler's assertion that reflection is commonly ignored or misunderstood in CSL is supported by at least one quantitative study
that found that only 4% of the projects investigated encouraged
reflective discourse between service recipients and providers; even
fewer of the projects (1%) actually implemented such reflective activity.[6]

All too often in CSL projects, though it's understood that reflection is paramount to success, there is a disinclination to implement structured reflective activities into those projects. This begs
an important question: why is reflection so often ignored in actual
practice? The disconnection between belief and implementation
seems to have a two-fold cause:

The activity of reflection is so familiar that, as teachers or trainers, we
often overlook it in formal learning settings, and make assumptions
about the fact that not only is it occurring, but it is occurring effectively
for everyone in the group. It is easy to neglect as it is something which
we cannot directly observe and which is unique to each learner.[7]

Second, because human beings come into the world with the ability to reflect on a limited, instinctual level, there is an unfounded
belief that no further training in how to reflect is necessary:

The basic reflective and puzzling techniques that help us make sense of
everyday life form the core of the very same techniques that enable students to derive meaningful learning from the experience of service; [how-
ever,] it is the critical questioning of why things are and the attempt to
fully understand the root causes of observable events and behaviors [that
must be taught]. This depth of critical reflection grows out of the instinctual reflective process but must be cultivated purposefully as a habit of
the mind.[8]

Patrick Whitaker has observed that by the time children are of
school age, "they have exercised their huge learning potential in

myriad ways to become sturdy individuals, with the skill of adaptation, self-management and communication already well established."[9] All too often students are assumed to have critical, reflective skills, and therefore structured, reflective instruction and practice are ignored in both planning and implementation of CSL projects. Quality CSL simply cannot happen without a clear understanding of what reflection is and how it must be taught, modeled, and practiced. This understanding, therefore, must be actively and consciously incorporated into any CSL project regardless of the ability or experience that participating students *seem* to have.

The Relationship among Community, Service, Academics, and Reflection

At the beginning of this chapter, I suggested that the process of reflection and its relationship to community, service and academics must be understood for CSL to succeed. An analysis of reflection makes clear the nature of this necessary relationship. As Eyler, Giles, and Schmiede argue, reflection is "contextual."[10] This contextual nature best explains how reflection connects academics to service within community. In CSL projects, academic, classroom learning provides an introduction to the skills needed for solving a community problem; the service project is the problematic context in which academic learning is applied and thereby learned. This in itself is nothing new, particularly in light of experiential learning theory and practice. However, it is only through reflection properly understood and practiced that students, teachers, and community members decide *how* academics might be applied to the community problem. Reflection brings academics to the service experience by contemplating the question, "How can classroom learning be applied to transform this particular communal problematic situation?" Conversely, a teacher might consider, "How can this problematic situation transform classroom learning?" Without the connection provided through reflective thought, the depth of learning that is hoped for in CSL simply will not come to pass (once again a telling shortcoming of the PARKnership project).

The contextual nature of reflection is explained by the fact that it is the result of a felt problem. As such, reflection requires that individuals step back from the problem and construct hypotheses about how academic knowledge/skills might be applied to fix or reconstruct the problem situation. These hypotheses are then tested in the problem situation and judged for success and failure. Only when reflection has all of these features can it bring community, service, and academics together to create learning and solve the community problem. CSL practice succeeds only when it embraces this very specific relationship among experience, academics, community, and reflection. John Dewey's notion of reflective thought explains how this necessary relationship might best be understood in CSL projects.

Deweyan Reflection

Humans are born with an inherent rudimentary ability to reflect in a trial-and-error fashion, and the story of that reflective ability parallels the history of the human species. As a concept, the history of reflection can be traced back at least as far as the writing of Aristotle.[11] However, the more recent work of John Dewey, as pointed out below, most completely explains how reflection might best be conceptualized in contemporary CSL practice:

> Dewey (1933) crystallized what many generations of teachers had known and practiced intuitively, namely that there were two kinds of experiential processes which led to learning. The first process was trial and error, which led to "rule of thumb" decisions. The value to the learner of this kind of process was limited by the specificity of the problem which was solved and the scope of the trial and error explorations. The second process he identified was reflective activity, which involved the perception of relationships, and connections between the parts of an experience. Dewey believed that it was this kind of activity that enabled effective problem-solving to take place and that it improved the effectiveness of learning.[12]

David Cooper writes:

> Dewey (1933) presents one of the most durable cases, as Kolb (1984) acknowledges, for the critical primacy of structured reflective thinking in the educative process. Dewey argues that reflective thinking is both the means and end that should be cultivated by education, properly considered.[13]

Certainly, John Dewey is not the only educational philosopher to map out the workings of reflection and thought. As I explained in Chapter Three, though CSL-like practices have been around for more than a century, CSL as a specific educational philosophy has been in existence only since the early 1970s. In the last 40 years, much has been written about what reflection is and how it should be practiced. One often-cited example is found, once again, in the work of David Kolb. Kolb is helpful in reminding readers what Dewey said about the process of reflection and, therefore, learning. However, as one critic correctly laments:

> Kolb does not discuss the nature of his stage of observation and reflection in much detail. His scheme has been useful in assisting us in planning learning activities and in helping us check simply that learners can be effectively engaged by the tasks we have set. It does not help, however, to uncover the elements of reflection itself.[14]

And, as I argued in the previous chapter, Kolb's account of experiential learning and reflection are overly reductionist at best, and contribute to the repression critical theorists warn of, at its worst. Kolb is one prominent proponent of CSL among many who have attempted to map out the reflective process; and yet, they are all more or less indebted to the work of Dewey.[15] Given the indebtedness to Dewey's understanding of reflection, I believe it best to go straight to the proverbial horse's mouth.

The Features of Reflection

Dewey suggested that thinking could be understood in several different ways. It is first discernable as conscious thought that, try as we may, we cannot stop. It is this type of thought that William James described as the "flights and perchings" of consciousness.[16] Thought also is found in fancy and imagination. Story making falls into this second category and is characterized not by the quest for knowledge or problem solution, but as an emotive expression that has as its goal an interesting plot or surprising climax. Belief is the third kind of thought described by Dewey. Belief is built up through "tradition, instruction, [and] imitation."[17] Belief is based on "prejudgments," not on examinations of evidence. And it is belief, often unexamined and dogmatic, that is antithetical to reflection and that is often the source of self and institutional repression.

Finally, Dewey talked of formal, scientific thinking, which is problem oriented—what he called "reflective thought." Reflective thought is "active, persistent, and careful consideration of any belief or supposed form of knowledge in the light of the grounds that support it and the further conclusions to which it tends."[18] It is reflective thinking that Dewey was most concerned with, and reflective thinking, as Dewey described it, is what brings together CSL community projects and academic, classroom skills to create learning situations in community. And it is reflective thought that can drive increasingly stronger versions of CSL projects, projects done with an eye to restructuring selves and institutions.

Dewey provided contemporary CSL educators with a clear foundation for fomenting reflection in their students. He explained that reflective thought has specific features that can be understood by disentangling them conceptually from the actual process:

> So much for the general features of a reflective experience. They are (i) perplexity, confusion, doubt, due to the fact that one is implicated in an incomplete situation whose full character is not yet determined; (ii) a conjectural anticipation—a tentative interpretation of the given elements, attributing to them a tendency to effect certain consequences; (iii) a careful survey (examination, inspection, exploration, analysis) of all attainable consideration which will define and clarify the problem in hand; (iv) a consequent elaboration of the tentative hypothesis to make it more precise and more consistent, because squaring with a wider range of facts; (v) taking one stand upon the projected hypothesis as a plan of action which is applied to the existing state of affairs: doing something overtly to bring about the anticipated result, and thereby testing the hypothesis.[19]

This conceptual outline of reflection should not be viewed as a regulated, four- or five-step program, or stop and go cycle, that leads to reflective Nirvana—certainly a danger given his analytical approach to its description above. Numerous writers who support CSL particularly, and experiential learning generally, seem to forget that Dewey's discussion is a means to understand what is in reality a rather sophisticated and intricate process.[20] To view the process is to see complicated meanderings from problem to hypothesis to past experience to testing, and back and forth. That means that individual students may be at different reflective places, doing somewhat different things, at different times. Though this makes a teacher's work even more complicated, it is the nature of reflective thought.

"Felt Problems" as Catalysts to Reflection

The first feature of reflective thought that must be understood in CSL is its initiating cause. Reflective thought comes about because an experience causes a "state of doubt, hesitation, perplexity, mental difficulty" in individual students.[21] I have suggested numerous times that I believe it essential to CSL particularly (and education generally) that learning be driven by problems in student experience. When one looks at what reflection entails, it becomes acutely clear why student interest and purpose are essential.

Reflective thought occurs only when a truly felt problem (one vitally important enough to cause perplexing uneasiness) is discovered, found, stumbled upon, or guided to. If a problem does not come out of student experience—if it is fabricated by another, or is not genuinely felt by the student—there will be no catalyst to reflection. And without reflection, there are no contextual connections to be made between classroom learning and the experience itself: there is no learning, much less transformative reconstruction of self and situation.

It also is essential to successful CSL practice to understand the emotive nature of problems, both as catalysts and aims of reflection. The realization of a problem comes about as an affective, rather than a cognitive, feeling that something is amiss as Robert R. Sherman suggested in Chapter Two.[22] Dewey writes about this initiating stage of thought that

> The difficulty may be *felt* with sufficient definiteness as to set the mind at once speculating upon its probable solution, or an undefined *uneasiness* and *shock* may come first, leading only later to definite attempt to find out what is the matter.[23]

CSL teachers must understand that projects, to be successful, can come only from students' feeling a direct emotional attachment to the service problem. In this way, the service itself, through reflective connection to academic study, can accomplish educationally sound aims. Without it, there is no problem to be solved and no context for the application of academic, classroom-acquired abilities.

Not only does the affective realization of a problem initiate thought, it also necessarily drives the entire reflective process. Because the initiator of thought is a perplexity, uneasiness, shock, or incompleteness in experience, the goal of reflection is to close that uneasiness, a reconstruction of the experience that brings organic emotional unity to it once again. As Dewey argued, "The two limits of every unit of thinking are a perplexed, troubled, or confused situation at the beginning and a cleared-up, unified, resolved situation at the close."[24] Reflective scrutiny, when driven by student interest and purpose, demands the application of classroom academics to resolve the felt community-service-project problem.

In bringing academic skills learned in the classroom to the service project, purposeful activity (such as advocated by William Kilpatrick) in the form of knowledge and skills are brought to a genuinely felt problem in a student's experience. In this way, the particular knowledge and skills are practiced, honed, and critiqued for success and adjustment within the service project activity. The service-project experience and academic learning are intimately bound together through reflection by asking and answering such questions as "what can be done together, using the skills learned in this classroom within this school, to solve this important community problem?" The result is the reinforcement in experience of academic learning as well as the formation of participatory, interactive/transactional democratic habits.

The Mediation of a Felt Problem

As an emotional, affective activity, problem detection is, in and of itself, instinctual and involuntary rather than reflective. If humans simply felt and immediately reacted, they would be as any creature on earth, acting simply on instinct. However, the second, third, and fourth of Dewey's "features of reflective thought" replace instinctual reaction with thoughtful mediation:

> To be genuinely thoughtful, we must be willing to sustain and protract that state of doubt which is the stimulus to thorough inquiry, so as not to accept an idea or make positive assertion of a belief until justifying reasons have been found.[25]

Reflective patience is the most important feature of reflection proper, and most essential to teach students participating in a CSL project. It is an important educational aim in and of itself. The mediating feature of reflection is where reasoning occurs and where answers to the question "What can we do to solve this community problem?" are initially considered. This stepping back and away from the situation is necessary to the reflective process. Avoidance of snap judgments, or unreasoned or reactionary attempts to solve problems is the hallmark of reflection. This mediation is what distinguishes reflective thought from instinctual reaction.

It is also during mediating a problem that plans for problem solution are turned over in the mind, discussed, and hypotheses are formed:

> The object of thinking is to help reach a conclusion, to project a possible termination on the basis of what is already given. Certain other facts about thinking accompany this feature. Since the situation in which thinking occurs is a doubtful one, thinking is a process of inquiry, of looking into things, of investigating.[26]

The ultimate goal of problem mediation is to develop a hypothesis that, once applied, will bring a reconstruction of the situation to make it complete and satisfying once again—thereby, once again, reconstructing self and situation. That is, mediation as a reflective feature provides the time and consideration to develop academic solutions to the service problem.

Reflection after Mediation: Hypothesis Testing

Testing hypotheses involves two important steps. Initially, hypotheses are formulated and go through a "mental testing." Through mental testing, possible consequences are considered for each plan and those that are found lacking in one way or another, are discarded. Once one hypotheses or plan is chosen, it must go through a second, decisive stage of testing. In this testing of the hypotheses, it is applied to the project problem, and experience (as is maintained in the previous chapter of this study) becomes both the means and the ends of CSL. That is, to be educative, CSL must begin and end with student experience. If it does not, then the purposeful nature of student interest will not drive learning. This means that ideas about how best to solve a felt problem must be tested in student experience. In describing this feature of reflection, Dewey explained that the

> concluding and conclusive step is some kind of experimental corroboration, or verification, of the conjectural idea. Reasoning shows that if the idea be adopted, certain consequences follow. So far the conclusion is hypothetical or conditional. If we look and find the characteristic traits

called for by rival alternatives to be lacking, the tendency to believe, to accept, is almost irresistible. If it is found that the experimental results agree with the theoretical, or rationally deduced, results, and if there is reason to believe that only the conditions in question would yield such results, the confirmation is so strong as to induce a conclusion.[27]

Hypotheses developed through reflective thought must be tested in experience. In the particular case of CSL, reasoned "guesses" about how to transform the community problem are applied and then evaluated for their success or failure. The community problem is then reevaluated and the process continues until reconstruction brings back the initially lost emotional equilibrium. The hypothesis-testing feature of reflective thought shows the involved students exactly how their hypotheses worked out. The students learn through experience. By testing these reasoned hypotheses, academic skills learned in theory become experientially real and transformative to both self and situation.

Reflection as Continual Component of CSL Projects

As Eyler says and Dewey implied, reflection must be a continual component of any CSL project. Reflection, as explained by Dewey, is an unending cycling from experience to mediation to testing to experience that cannot be ignored before, during, or after a service project. Eyler, Giles, and Schmiede make clear that "reflection should maintain an especially coherent continuity over the course of each event or experience. Continuous reflection includes reflection before the experience, during the experience and after the experience."[28] James and Pamela Toole write that "although the literal definition of reflection means 'looking backward,' reflection occurs at every phase of the service-learning cycle: reflection to prepare for service, reflection during action, and reflection upon action."[29] Exactly how reflection can and should be maintained before, during, and after service projects is a crucial issue to the success of CSL—one that often is ignored or left only for post-service activities—once again, think PARKnership project.

Reflection before Practice: "Preflection"

According to Diane Falk, "preflection" is the reflective preparation that occurs before the actual service project begins.[30] Boud, Keogh, and Walker point out that during preflection, "students start to explore what is required of them, what are the demands of the field setting and the resources which they themselves have to bring."[31] It is a chance for students to imagine what the experience will be like and to express concerns related to the project.[32] Preflection is a concept that reminds CSL educators that reflection must be continual. It also adds to Dewey's analysis of reflection by indicating the preparation needed, both emotionally and cognitively, to engage in community problem-solving service.

However, preparatory reflection as described above is missing an essential Deweyan element: student involvement in project choice. Boud, Keogh, and Walker assume that a project has already been chosen without input from the students who will carry out the project. I believe this is a serious and unfortunately regular flaw in reflective theory and CSL implementation—and it's one I was guilty of in designing the PARKnership project described in Chapter One. For students to involve themselves in a project wholeheartedly and with purpose and interest, the project absolutely must come out of the felt interests of those students. As argued above, the feeling of a crucial community problem is the catalyst to reflection, and therefore must be genuinely felt to create a learning situation. That felt interest must be part of the "preflective" stage of project reflection. Combining Deweyan felt interest with the preparatory character of preflection makes it a complete and helpful notion to reflective theory and, therefore, to CSL practice.

James and Pamela Toole elaborate the above shortcoming in reflective theory when they explain their view of project preparation:

> Reflection *before* service may seem a contradiction, but we commonly reflect on and use prior knowledge and experience when we plan and design any project. In preparing for service work, students recollect, propose, hypothesize, build models, predict and make judgments. Students reflect when they choose a service project (*What do we wish were different in our community?*); when they clarify project goals and action plans (*What do we want to see happen?*); and when they prepare for the service itself (*How do we feel about participating in this project?*).[33]

The point cannot be overstated: the "preflective" stage of reflection must include project choice, planning, and rationale, or else the project will be doomed from the beginning. If the students do not choose the project out of a felt interest, then it will suffer from the artificiality found in traditional educational approaches.

Dewey was also clear to say that reflection, as described here, does not imply leaving students to their own means hoping they stumble upon a problem of interest.[34] What preflection does entail is a reformulation of the teacher's role. Instead of being a purveyor of already established knowledge, as in the "banking system" criticized by Paulo Freire (and unfortunately institutionalized NCLB), a teacher must be a guide who leads students to feel and realize problematic situations. Leading students to problems in experience is not an easy task. It includes the use of many traditional modes of teaching (reading great works and contemporary literature, for example) as well as more nontraditional practices, including going into one's community to see firsthand what's happening. Interacting with the community entails meeting community strangers and talking to them about community issues. It also means that student experience is the source of project choice. And importantly, it means blurring the line between school and community, as suggested previously. CSL educators must be mindful that

> Only learners themselves can learn and only they can reflect on their own experiences. Teachers can intervene in various ways to assist, but they only have access to individuals' thoughts and feelings through what individuals choose to reveal about themselves.[35]

In addition to project choice and interest, preflection must be a time for project preparation as well. Once the students discover a problem, the reflective process is in full swing. It will naturally incorporate previous experience and, more importantly, indicate lack of previous experience. This will be particularly true when students meet community strangers—those fellow citizens who have firsthand knowledge of the realized problem. The preflective stage, as is pointed out above, must include expressing emotions and clarifying assumptions about the problem and about those citizens who regularly experience that problem. It will involve some guessing as to outcomes, roles, and further problems. It will, in short, be the catalyst and, as Dewey says, "the steadying and guiding factor" for the project.[36]

Reflection during Service

Reflection is an ongoing process and though preparatory reflection (preflection) is essential to project implementation, much, if not most, critical reflection in CSL occurs during the project work. Reflection during the project drives academic learning as the hypotheses developed for solving the project problem are tested, adjusted through further data gathering, re-applied, and re-tested. Reflection provides the opportunity for learning in that it brings the service problem and classroom together in the context of the project. Applying classroom learning in the project context "teaches" academic understanding well beyond traditional classroom settings, because the students use classroom-constructed knowledge and skills to solve real problems. Students, side by side with community members who have a stake in the service problem, make project decisions. Students operating in the project context create knowledge and sharpen academic skills as they solve present and future community problems. The project context also leads to better reflective skills as students make project decisions and test those decisions for success or failure.

CSL calls for continual reflection that not only develops academic/reflective skills, but connects disparate community groups as well. That is, service, as it's understood in Chapter Six, is an interactive experience. There I argued that too often the "served" are not consulted prior to or during project work. In order to create community connections, as called for in the concepts of community and service, reflective activities must involve all stakeholders. In particular, students and affected community members must discuss project decisions and effects through structured reflection. Only in interactive, structured reflection can good project decisions be made and democratic connections maintained. Clearly this is another important way that reflection, when understood and practiced correctly, connects academics to community service by including all interested parties in meaningful, democratic dialogue, and is reflective of the community theory suggested in Chapter Five.

The reflective dialogue required in CSL projects will bind students to community members and academics to experience only if it is structured with both cognitive and affective goals in mind:

> Reflection as we have described it is pursued with intent. It is not idle meanderings or day-dreaming, but purposive activity directed towards a

goal. This is not to say that it may not be helpful to have periods of reverie and mediation associated with conscious reflection, but in themselves these activities are not what we are referring to when we discuss goal-directed critical reflection. The reflective process is a complex one in which both feelings and cognition are closely interrelated and interactive. Negative feelings, particularly about oneself, can form major barriers towards learning. They can distort perceptions, lead to false interpretations of events, and can undermine the will to persist. Positive feelings and emotions can greatly enhance the learning process; they can keep the learner on the task and can provide a stimulus for new learning. The affective dimension has to be taken into account when we are engaged in our own learning activities, and when we are assisting others in this process.[37]

Clearly, the idea that reflection is easy, or at least instinctual, is a misperception. The reflective process, as it is embraced here, is continual and should be taught by modeling and structuring it with specific goals in mind and even itself reflected upon.

The actual form that continual project reflection takes can and should vary according to student interest and levels of development. Eyler, Giles, and Schmiede argue that in order to take advantage of differing learning styles, for example, a wide variety of reflective approaches should be used, including directed discussion, journaling, oral presentations, and role playing.[38] The Pennsylvania Institute for Environmental and Community Service Learning advocates reflection that is structured around four modes of communication: reading, writing, talking, and observing objects.[39] James and Pamela Toole suggest the use of the "What? So what? Now what?" cycle based on the work of David Kolb.[40] These structured forms of reflection, as well as others, can be successful, but only if the features of the reflective process discussed here are carried through each reflective experience. Reflection must be driven by the essential goal of any CSL project: to reconstruct the situation to bring a resolution to the felt problem, therein entailing both community- and self-reconstruction. Reflection guided by this idea will promote cognitive, emotional, and even physical learning during the project, as adjustments are discussed and made in order to form better hypotheses and applied plans of action.

Post-Project Reflection: A Continuation, Not a Culmination

Reflection means to look back, so it is most commonly practiced when projects are over. As James and Pamela Toole remark, "In the aftermath of a project, students therefore need to formally reflect in order to evaluate the project, assess their own development, look for generalizations to guide future decision making and find 'new applications' for what they have learned."[41] In the case of American education, more often than not this is seen as an end to the particular project and as a culmination of a semester or year-long course. Certainly it is crucial that reflective discourse carry into the post-project period. However, seeing post-project reflection as the final act in the project context is clearly a misunderstanding of Deweyan reflective features. Instead of the project ending when the CSL course ends, reflective practice (when understood correctly) requires that the project problem be re-examined by all stakeholders, together. In this way, democratic communal interaction and evaluation is maintained and encouraged, and project success is evaluated through continuing reflection.

The reflective post-project examination will determine the successes and failures of the problem solutions. It will also indicate future and related problems with the project context or in similar contexts. It is therefore paramount to construct and implement project activities based on the idea that the project is over only when a satisfactory reconstruction of, or solution to, the problem has been achieved. Until that time, the project will continue in new and different ways, with new and different insights. Post-project reflection is simply another case of stepping back from the situation to see the degree to which project activities have solved the initial problem. It's a time for bringing together both project impact and learning with an eye to future similar experiences.

On an individual basis, Deweyan theory, as well as the community service structure advocated here, asks each student involved in the project to continue reflecting on the problem situation. It requires that upon ending the course, graduating, or moving on in some other way, students take both the general reflective skills and the knowledge of the particular community problem with them. It also asks them to apply those skills to similar community situations. In this way, the reflective cycle generally and the problem situation particularly lead to similar work in the individual's later experience. CSL done well will create continuity through opening new and related experiences from those of the past, and in so doing, the students involved continue to grow through pursuing similar such experiences—the definition of an educative experience.

Reflective Practice: A Note on Specific Activities

There is a tendency among CSL advocates to regard reflection as simply "fun" activities that allow students to look back in celebration at what their service project has accomplished. In fact, grant recipients are often encouraged to include celebratory activities following the completion of a project, and these activities often look reflective in nature.[42] However, reflection, understood as it is presented here, is a serious activity without which CSL will not work at all. Volumes have been published listing activities for reflection and commenting on the value of such activities.[43] Suggested activities are wide and varied in both structure and degrees of success. Group discussion, role playing, writing, acting, presenting, and debating activities all might lead to good reflective practice.

These activities, however, do not in and of themselves satisfy the reflective requirement I suggest here for CSL education. The success of each such activity will be found in whether or not it leads the student to reflect in the manner described above. Does the activity lead students to see a problem in their experience? Does the activity make students step back from a problem to plan a solution? Does the activity get students to apply their academic learning to possible solutions? Does the activity lead students to test that plan in the problem situation? Does the activity bring students to a re-evaluation of the problem situation and those similar to it? Does the activity involve dialogue among all stakeholders? Does the activity encourage further reflection? Does the activity result in individual and communal transformation? Regardless of what the reflective activity specifically entails, if it is not structured in such a way to answer the above questions in the affirmative, then it is not reflective in nature and cannot be a part of CSL education.

Implications for Practice

I suggested initially in this chapter that reflection is the tie that binds community-service activity to academics in a CSL project. Reflection gives students the opportunity to apply classroom learning in a meaningful community project. This application of knowledge to experience leads to learning that goes well beyond traditional educational practices. Not only are academic skills sharpened, but democratic notions of community and connection are developed as well. As such, reflective theory has clear consequences for CSL practice. Foremost among them is the implication such understanding has for the role of the teacher.

Reflection strengthens the notion that a teacher's role in CSL is not to give information and expect students simply to repeat it on a test. Instead, CSL is student centered, and the teacher's roles are as guide, mentor, and model. In the role of guide, the teacher leads students (because of her greater depth and breadth of experience) to and through troubling experiences, thereby aiding in the construction of new knowledge. Such a teacher must be open-minded and diligent in the face of difficult and disquieting questions that might cause student doubt and challenge deeply held beliefs.

As a mentor, a teacher must work intimately with her students as they deal with their own personal challenges as well as the challenges brought by project implementation. The CSL teacher has to maintain the difficult balancing act of being both mentor and participant. She cannot, as is the case so often in traditional classrooms, separate herself from what the students are doing. She also must understand how reflective practice works and the impact it can have on student development. She must teach students how to reflect by structuring and participating in activities that will give them the opportunity to use their reflective, academic, and social skills in experience. In this way, she will be able to see her students through academic and dispositional learning that comes out of student experience and leads back to it—and this kind of community and self-transformative teaching is difficult indeed. The CSL teacher should remain mindful that in CSL projects, as a model she is relied upon for developing reflective thought, which requires being clear to her students about how reflection works and continually modeling and explaining it.

Reflection has clear consequences for all community members as well. Above all else, reflective thought is a problem-solving activity. Felt problems on the part of students are rarely if ever confined to the school walls. Student problems are community problems, and therefore demand the participation of the entire community if they are to be solved. Reflective theory requires that a dialogue occur among all community stakeholders and that all stakeholders understand their roles in solving the problem. Only through broad reflective dialogue and action can CSL be the re-connecting community practice that is called for in sound theory.

Finally, reflection in CSL has consequences for the way academic gains should be measured. Experience rather than abstraction becomes the source of academic/cognitive and affective/emotional transformative learning. However, it is only through reflecting on that experience in a structured manner that experiential learning can be retained and transferred to similar experiences. Student experience, as Dewey argued, is both the means and aims of education.[44] Only by mediating and reflecting on that experience, in this case the CSL project, can students become better equipped to deal with present and future problem situations. Reflection reminds educators that learning is not simply a matter of mastering information, but involves the use of cognitive skills attained in CSL. That idea must be kept at the forefront of any evaluation of student progress.

The connection between community experience and formal education that reflection provides—and that I advocate here—could become a powerful reform for both P–12 and higher education in this country. CSL as I have conceptualized it here requires the reassessment of teacher and student roles, community relationships, and community participation. This reassessment could radically change how education is currently practiced and might lead to a more-informed and participatory public, and ultimately to a stronger democracy. CSL might, in fact, become the source for investigating democratic institutions, adjusting those institutions, and in so doing make schools a source for reconstructing society more generally. The degree to which this reconstructive possibility exists is, I believe, to be found in the degree to which CSL projects are relatively weaker or stronger.

CHAPTER NINE

Democratic Education: Weak Community Service Learning

Introduction

In the two ensuing chapters, this one and the next, I will leave the consideration of the internal workings of CSL and make two claims about it in terms of its broader external potential, both of which I have hinted at throughout the earlier chapters. The first of these, and the topic of the present chapter, is that CSL, particularly as I have envisioned its conceptual structure in preceding chapters, is the epitome of democratic pedagogy—one that is democratic in its means and one whose overarching aim is the extension of democratic habits of action from and through schools into the broader community; and one entailed in the conception of community outlined in Chapter Five. I call this "weak" CSL not because it has little or no value—it certainly does, but because it falls a bit short of what I believe is CSL's full critical potential.

This first claim is important for two reasons, one that is not so new and the other only somewhat so. First, our country has, in theory if not always in practice, developed around general democratic notions, and its system of public education exists in part as an essential institution for strengthening the philosophical understanding of the democratic social ideal alluded to in Chapter Five—this is the not-so-new idea.[1] Secondly, the strong version of CSL that I will suggest in the next chapter comes directly from the first: in its strong form CSL has the radical potential to reconstruct individuals, communities and institutional structures that are currently oppressive—a claim that I cannot make if CSL is not first defended in its weak version as a democratic pedagogy

In its weak version, CSL is a reform rather than a radical departure from current practice or an educational revolution that would fundamentally change the way public education (or other institutions) operates in this country. As an educational reform rather than a paradigmatic revolution, CSL is simultaneously constrained by institutional policy while obligated to develop deeper democratic understanding even as its advocates re-form, re-shape, or re-work specific educational practices. Mainstream (or traditional) CSL educators and their students do not typically seek to analyze and reconstruct those underlying institutional structures. In fact, from what I've seen at my institution, CSL projects more typically extend or lend support to those existing (often oppressive) structures in projects manifested out of rather weak conceptual understandings of community, service, learning, and reflection. On the other hand, there is much to be said for CSL's democratic potential, and without that, it certainly cannot evolve into the more radicalized strong version that it might become.

With all of this in mind, I will suggest some general characteristics that are basic to any understanding of democratic education. I will briefly examine these characteristics and then use them to place CSL within a somewhat mainstream, democratically oriented educational context. In doing so, I address the important question of whether this weak version of CSL meets the most basic demands of a democratic theory of education, and if so, how it does so. Placing CSL theory and practice within a broader democratic educational understanding should allow it to become a critical tool for evaluating CSL projects (such as my PARKnership project) as a minimally democratic undertaking, and can provide the essential requirements needed from which a strong version of CSL might be built.

The Need for a Democratic Theory of Education

It is important to remember that educational practice does not occur in a social vacuum. In fact, as has been implicitly maintained throughout this study, education is essentially a social endeavor that aims to achieve valuable social ends. John Dewey argued that education is so important to a society that social philosophy itself might be correctly understood as the general theory of education.[2] Educational practice is the milieu in which important social ideas are tested, and their worth evaluated. This is particularly true in the United States, where public education is regularly criticized (though rarely praised) for its role as purveyor of democratic ideals and engine for the American economy.[3] Democratic education's overarching aim is the perpetuation of what

Seymour Lipset Jr. calls America's exceptional "democratic creed."[4]

John Dewey argued in *Democracy and Education* that democracy as generally understood in the United States best enables citizens to interact across social classes—classes that were, until relatively recently, purposefully organized so as to remain only vaguely connected one to another.[5] This social class separation came in the form of an aristocratic social construct that used physical force and birth obligation, rather than shared interests and interaction, as tools for social control. As I suggested in Chapter Five, this construct has been supported historically in part by oppressive conceptions of service, the needy, and the myth of the American Dream. Democracy, however (theoretically speaking), turns this hierarchical structure on its head by embracing give-and-take connection among individuals from every walk of life rather than disconnection perpetuated through class division and preestablished class responsibility. Dewey described democracy as a social ideal that is characterized by "varied points of shared common interest, [and] greater reliance upon the recognition of mutual interests as a factor in social control" that changes social habit in its demand for "continuous readjustment through meeting the new situations produced by varied intercourse."[6]

As the social ideal upon which America is founded, democracy must be the theoretical basis for educational practice as well. The understanding of public education in this country as the process through which the democratic social ideal is learned, reconstructed, and transmitted to future generations is essential to any educational practice. Clearly, if it is to be truly democratic, an educational practice such as CSL must be imbued with this exceptional democratic creed from start to finish:

> A society which makes provision for participation in its good of all its members on equal terms and which secures flexible readjustment of its institutions through interaction of the different forms of associated life is in so far democratic. Such a society must have a type of education which gives individuals a personal interest in social relationships and control, and the habits of mind which secure social changes without introducing disorder.[7]

Furthermore, as Amy Gutmann maintains in her important book *Democratic Education*, it is crucial that educational decisions be made via deliberative reflection rather by habitual knee-jerk reactions to public concerns in practice.[8] Similarly, William James described philosophical theory as visionary, or "prospective."[9] That is, without a philosophical position from which to direct practice, the path to achieving a good life through democratic education may consist of pendulum swings rather than reasonable, deliberative prospective decisions. Gutmann argues that in not developing and utilizing an educational *theory* on which to base practice,

> we neglect educational alternatives that may be better than those to which we have become accustomed or that may aid us in understanding how to improve our schools before we reach the point of crisis, when our reactions are likely to be less reflective because we have so little time to deliberate.[10]

Even in its weak version, CSL must meet the minimal requirements of democratic educational theory for it to pass muster as an acceptable American pedagogy.

The General Characteristics of a Democratic Theory of Education

Asserting that democratic educational practice is essential to the life of a democracy is quite different than characterizing precisely what a democratic education should entail, or judging a pedagogy's value in extending democratic habits of action. I believe that for any pedagogy to meet the bare minimums required of democratic education, it must be steeped in and simultaneously encourage in its students, teachers and the broader community, reflective-deliberation, social activism, nondiscriminaton, and nonrepression from an informed perspective. This perspective must be encouraged in students, teachers, and community members.

Democratic Education as Reflectively Deliberative, Informed, and Socially Active

A general democratic theory of education has three essential, inexorably connected characteristics that represent the theoretical basics for any educational practice operating in a democracy. First, democratic education must be reflective, as John Dewey maintained, and deliberative, as Amy Gutmann explained. That is, for an educational practice to be democratic in nature, it should champion reflective deliberation as a means of democratic participation and as a self-perpetuating end in itself. If an educational practice does not do so, then we as citizens are left without the most essential skill needed to participate in democratic decisions.

Reflection is taken here to be explicitly Deweyan. As is explained in Chapter Eight, the reflective process must be understood, modeled, practiced, and put to use correctly and continually if there is to be any expectation for students to learn it as a skill and as a general disposition. Educational practice must engender the most democratic of abilities, the ability to reflect and act upon problems in experience. Because democracy takes as its starting point the fact of diverse, thoughtful citizens as public-policy makers, those policy-making citizens must feel, mediate, and act on problems as they occur in their personal experience. Democracy is both appealing in its freedom and equally frightening in its faith that individual citizens can and will participate in public-policy decisions. In order to safeguard against the very real danger of democratic tyranny, the public justifiably expects its educational system to encourage young citizens to direct their activities "with foresight" and "plan according to ends-in-view or purposes" of which they are aware.[11]

In like fashion, because democracy is not anarchy, nor is it rule by experts, individual citizens must connect with one another to make decisions together. In Amy Gutmann's words, individuals must "deliberate" (publicly reflect) together as interested stakeholders, to make decisions that might reasonably solve or prevent socially important and commonly felt problems—and this is certainly entailed in the concepts of community and service I suggested earlier.

This democratic form of public-policy making will naturally lead to emotionally charged disagreements. Gutmann correctly maintains that these disagreements constitute an essential democratic virtue:

> The most distinctive feature of a democratic theory of education is that it makes a democratic virtue out of our inevitable disagreement over educational [and other] problems. The democratic virtue, too simply stated, is that we can publicly debate educational problems in a way much more likely to increase our understanding of education and each other than if we were to leave the management of schools, as Kant suggests, 'to depend entirely upon the judgment of the most enlightened experts.' The policies that result from our democratic deliberations will not always be the right ones, but they will be more enlightened—by the values and concerns of the many communities that constitute a democracy—than

those that would be made by unaccountable educational experts. We can
do better to try instead to find the fairest ways for reconciling our disagreements, and for enriching our collective life by democratically debating them.[12]

To ensure that disagreement remains a democratic virtue, citizens
must learn that reflective deliberation is part of the democratic
process, which can be taught best by educational approaches that
incorporate reflective deliberation into their practice.

Of course, reflective deliberation will operate at its best when
the public is informed in the traditional educational manner. That
is, the classically maintained educational aim of skills acquisition
and knowledge construction cannot be ignored. Academic aims are
crucial to CSL because the best action decisions come from an academically informed position. If they do not come from that position, they will not be wise decisions. Though, as Alfred North
Whitehead famously proclaimed, "A merely well-informed man is
the most useless bore on God's earth"; a merely reflective, yet un-
informed democrat might be the most dangerous person on God's
earth.[13] I have suggested that building knowledge and acquiring
skills can best be achieved by using ideas in practice—the experiential epistemology of the progressives discussed earlier. As
Whitehead also argued, "In training a child to activity of thought,
above all things we must beware of what I will call 'inert ideas'—
that is to say, ideas that are merely received into the mind without
being utilized, or tested, or thrown into fresh combinations."[14] A
knowledgeable reflective deliberator is a wise citizen who under-
stands her position deeply, expresses it clearly and often, and
knows when and how to act.

Finally, informed reflective deliberation can be democratic in
nature only when reasonable decisions are put to use in the democratic experience. Again, Whitehead's point is clear (and is supported in the work of many theorists discussed earlier). To be vital
to a student, knowledge, skills, and reflection must come from
lived experience and must then return to experience for testing.
William Kilpatrick built his philosophy of education on purposeful
activity; John Dewey championed mediation, hypothesizing, and
testing; and Paul Hanna suggested active community transformation through problem-solution. Each of these progressive scholars
characterizes educational practice as socially active. John Dewey
captures the nature of this relationship when he says that demo-

cratic "society must have a type of education which gives individuals a personal interest in social relationships and control, and the habits of mind which secure social change without introducing disorder."[15] At a bare minimum, students must have the opportunity to actively test hypotheses of action; at its strongest, CSL would encourage the action to be increasingly rugged, courageous, and public. The more engaged students, teachers, and community members are in a CSL project, the more potential there is for self- and community-transformation.

Democratic Education as Nonrepressive and Nondiscriminatory

Arguing from a position inspired by the work of John Dewey, Amy Gutmann provides two explicit additions to democratic educational theory—nonrepression and nondiscrimination.[16] She argues that although the above-mentioned general characteristics clearly are essential to understanding democratic education, they are not enough to defend against what Alex de Tocqueville described as the "tyranny of the majority" or what Gutmann might call the tyranny of the family.[17] These additional democratic characteristics—nonrepression and nondiscrimination—are important protectors of reflective, informed, and socially active deliberation. They prevent the possibility that democracy is transformed into a tyranny that stifles the voices and actions of marginalized groups or individuals. As educational notions that protect "conscious social reproduction," they provide future citizens with the same reflective rights and obligations as those enjoyed by current citizens.[18]

According to Gutmann:

> The principle of nonrepression prevents the state, and any group within it, from using education to restrict *rational* deliberation of competing conceptions of the good life and the good society. Nonrepression is not a principle of negative freedom. It secures freedom from interference only to the extent that it forbids using education to restrict rational deliberation or consideration of different ways of life. Nonrepression is therefore compatible with the use of education to inculcate those character traits, such as honesty, religious toleration, and mutual respect for persons, that serve as foundations for rational deliberation of differing ways of life. Nor is nonrepression a principle of positive liberty, as commonly understood. Although it secures more than a freedom from interference, the "freedom to" that it secures is not a freedom to pursue the singularly

correct way of personal or political life, but the freedom to deliberate rationally among differing ways of life. Because *conscious* social reproduction is the primary ideal of democratic education, communities must be prevented from using education to stifle rational deliberation of competing conceptions of the good life and the good society.[19]

As implied particularly in the community theory embraced earlier, and as I argue below, nonrepression is an essential characteristic of even weak CSL theory and is reflective of communal interaction/transaction; it must, however, be made explicit so that CSL practitioners will keep it ever mindful.

The second important addition Gutmann makes to democratic theory and, by implication, to CSL theory is the idea that democratic education must be nondiscriminatory. For public education to be democratic in the sense that all citizens ought to participate in the democratic process, it must be made available to every individual. Clearly, nondiscrimination is a distributional complement to nonrepression; that is, nondiscrimination is a universal democratic right. As Gutmann convincingly argues, repression historically has come in the form of hidden institutionalized classroom practices that ignore or stifle the voices and actions of such groups as women or racial minorities. Nondiscrimination attempts to eliminate the hidden marginalizing of minority groups by demanding that every individual have access to democratic education. This policy is meant to ensure that the skills necessary to reflective, informed, socially active deliberation are available for all educable students. Gutmann explains that

> nondiscrimination extends the logic of nonrepression, since states and families can be selectively repressive by excluding entire groups of children from schooling or by denying them an education conducive to deliberation among conceptions of the good life and the good society. In its most general application to education, nondiscrimination prevents the state, and all groups within it, from denying anyone an educational good on grounds irrelevant to the legitimate social purpose of that good. Applied to those forms of education necessary to prepare children for future citizenship (participation in conscious social reproduction), the nondiscrimination principle becomes a principle of nonexclusion. No educable child may be excluded from an education adequate to participating in the political processes that structure choice among good lives.[20]

These two principles, when added to informed, socially active, and reflective deliberation (conscious social reproduction), create a helpful understanding of democratic educational principles. When added to the conceptual understanding of CSL, they also establish a firm foundation upon which to develop future CSL activities in its weak version, to evaluate CSL projects in their level of basic democratic character, and form the basis from which a strong version of CSL might be built.

Weak CSL as a Democratic Educational Reform

The democratic characteristics discussed above, it must be reemphasized, represent the bare minimum that any form of democratic education must meet. The questions for CSL are, quite simply, can it meet these minimal requirements and how might it do so? Generally, CSL is a viable form of democratic education; however, like all educational approaches, it is one whose success is left to those individuals who organize and implement it. As I suggested from the outset, even in its weak version, for CSL to be democratically educative, its practitioners must have a minimal conceptual understanding of what is entailed in its practice.

CSL as Reflective-Deliberative, Informed, and Socially Active

As I argued in Chapter Eight, reflective activity is at the heart of CSL practice. In advocating reflection in CSL as Dewey conceived it, I suggest that reflection must be a continual activity throughout a CSL project. It should not simply be the post-project reflection as commonly practiced in CSL projects, including my own PARKnership program. Project choice comes out of student-felt problems; informed student plans are formulated; and those plans are then put to the test in the problem experience to evaluate their worth. Clearly, this type of reflection is required of any form of democratic education. Because democracy is based on individual participation in making public policy, citizens must have available the skills needed to mediate and reasonably consider problems of personal and public importance. Amy Gutmann's idea of deliberation—reflection made public—completes the notion of democratic participation as public-policy decisions. That is, individuals reflect and deliberate together to make democratic decisions—persuading, listening, deciding, and testing-by-acting.

The service aspect of CSL is part and parcel of reflective deliberation. In the service activity, student-made plans are put to the test in attempts to solve the project problem. More importantly, however, the service activity provides an important deliberative opportunity for the students carrying out the projects: they have the opportunity to speak to, deliberate with, learn from, connect, and act with a population of strangers. As is implied in Chapter Five, the real democratic work is done when groups of strangers come together, work together, solve problems together, and connect as people who have similarities as well as differences. This intense form of deliberative interaction meets the democratic demand for reflective-deliberative conscious social reproduction and creates a situation that is genuinely active and, therefore, educational. As project stakeholders make and act on contentious public decisions related to the service project, the democratic process is learned and gradually becomes a habitual form of social activity for all participants.

As a purely educational activity, CSL practitioners should use the project situation to aid in knowledge construction through active application of related skills. The decisions made and plans implemented through active reflection become the source for an increasingly complex understanding of knowledge and skills. This increased academic understanding does not mean that every plan is going to be successful in solving the project problem; to the contrary, testing, adjusting, and retesting new solutions in experience is what makes the learning in CSL so valuable and more powerfully democratic, in contrast to more traditional approaches. Informed, genuine decision making in service projects means that students develop skills and use ideas in ways that traditional, classroom-only education simply cannot match and in so doing become much more deeply knowledgeable democratic citizens.

Finally, even its weak form, CSL can be somewhat transformative for an entire community. As Paul Hanna argued and as is explained in a previous chapter, if the project problem is genuine and truly reflective-deliberative decisions are made and put into action, the community problem can be solved.[21] Ultimately, this community transformation activity is the epitome of education as a democratic endeavor. When the goal of community transformation/improvement is met through informed, reflective, and active citizen participation, education for democracy will have been achieved.

CSL as Nonrepressive and Nondiscriminatory

The two additional democratic components of nonrepression and nondiscrimination are more problematic for CSL. The reason they are more problematic is that, though they might be entailed in many of the various definitions of CSL, they are not explicitly stated or explained, as are its reflective-deliberative characteristics. As assumptions rather than stated democratic guiding principles, nonrepression and nondiscrimination remain unexplained and unexplored in CSL practice. It is simply assumed by CSL practitioners and theorists that both nonrepression and nondiscrimination will be a part of CSL practice, and it is in this assumption that some of its weak characteristics are sourced. However, as Gutmann makes clear, these democratic concepts must be made explicit if they are to be more than just vague, assumped and sometimes misunderstood guidelines for practice.

An example will clarify this concern. As I've noted several times in this study, there exist a seemingly endless number of definitions and guidelines for CSL practice. One of the more important events in CSL history was the creation of the Wingspread Special Report that contained "Ten Principles of Effective Service-Learning Practice." The last principle in that report is that an effective CSL program is "committed to program participation by and with diverse populations."[22] This particular characteristic of CSL practice is explained later in the report as an opportunity to "participate" with diverse people. However, it simply does not go far enough in explaining exactly what is meant by participation. As Richard Kraft points out,

> As the [Wingspread] report expands upon these principles, it continues to frame the involvement of service partners as service providers and recipients. As previously stated, this focus does not go far enough in acknowledging the strengths of the served, and does not adequately address the barriers keeping these individuals from fully participating in society. The concept of "partners in service" needs to be embraced in the principles themselves for programs to emulate a paragon of equality.[23]

This misguided notion of participant interaction can be corrected by the explicit inclusion of the principles of nonrepression and nondiscrimination as conceived by Amy Gutmann and in its service component as conceived by Howard Radest. These two democratic characteristics when combined with the service conception explained earlier demand that conversations among the strangers in a service project occur regularly and carry important meaning both in social connections and project problem solution. Without the explicit inclusion of nonrepression and nondiscrimination, CSL runs the risk of not satisfying the requirements demanded by a democratic form of public education. That demand is that all stakeholders have a voice in reflecting and acting to solve the project problem. To ensure that all voices are heard, nondiscrimination and nonrepression must be continually active policies that direct and protect reflective dialogue between served and server, doer and done to. When CSL is understood as socially active, reflective, deliberative, *and* when service is guided by the twin policies of nonrepression and nondiscrimination, it is a hopeful form of educational practice for the perpetuation of democracy through the creation of democratically minded, informed, and socially active citizens—it might, however, become something much more. I now turn my attention to the potential that a strong version of CSL might hold.

CHAPTER TEN

Toward Strong Community Service Learning

Introduction

Before getting to the specifics of what a strong version of CSL might look like, I want to make a couple of essential distinctions as to its place and practice in P–12 schools—initial distinctions that I believe will shed some light on its potential as a relatively stronger or weaker pedagogy of critical personal and communal transformation.

First, and as Dan Butin has suggested, CSL is "dangerous" on "pragmatic, political, and existential grounds." [1] I agree—and will simply add that danger typically and naturally breeds fear. On the other hand, danger is contextually relative, breeding contextually distinctive levels and types of fear. When the critical service-learning camp describes the dangerous revolutionary potential entailed in CSL, it is typically in the context of higher education, and often it seems, at private, rather prestigious, institutions.[2] This begs two questions: how revolutionary (or dangerous) can it really be given this context? And second, if it can transform relatively privileged students, professors, and institutions of higher learning, why can't it do the same for P–12 schools and underprivileged communities of place and interest?

I don't mean to imply that critical service learning theorists and pedagogues in higher education have nothing to say to P–12 teachers toiling in the context of increasingly impoverished rural and inner city schools—I believe they absolutely do. However, the perceived danger of CSL (particularly in its strong version) and the resulting fear is intensely real for administrators, teachers, students, and community members in the P–12 context, especially so relative to the lived experiences of professors (including myself these days) cloistered in the ivory tower of academia; and, especially so given the increasing systemic oppression of teachers via NCLB and RTTT. We must remain diligently mindful of this contextual difference because, as George Counts suggested, it is in and through the P–12 context—not the higher education context—that broad social justice aims can ultimately be achieved.

Second, though I do believe that critical theory provides proponents of CSL working in the P–12 context some valuable conceptual tools for incorporating it into practice (and argue so in advocating for strong CSL), I think that the typical American school teacher is understandably befuddled by its rather mysterious language (and the language of philosophers generally). I can attest to this firsthand: my students, pre-service and practicing teachers, get the most perplexed looks on their faces when we initially ponder such theory. They often seem to be holding in loud guffaws of professional astonishment (no doubt out of courtesy to their dear old professor). And, as I said early on, I remember feeling much the same way in my previous life as a high school English teacher. In advocating for a strong version of CSL, I hope to demystify some of that language and in so doing help to make it practical for the P–12 context.

Finally, I want to point out a distinction between critical theory and critical pedagogy (recently suggested by my colleague Jessica Heybach…thank you, Jessica)—one that hints at the difference in weak and strong conceptions of CSL. This distinction is reflective of the essential problem manifested in the understanding of community as outlined in Chapter Five (and put into play in each of the ensuing chapters): that of the historic dualism between the inward and the outward.[3] As I hope to make clear below, critical theory traditionally has its eye on macro-cultural issues—an outward orientation toward the analysis and elimination of systemic institutional oppression. Critical pedagogy, as the practical manifestation of critical theory, is more typically about the transformation of self, and rarely makes the critical turn toward the outward, toward acting for institutional change, particularly in CSL projects. Maybe an example can help us visualize this distinction.

A prototypically common CSL project is having students spend some time at the local community homeless shelter providing some kind of service, often the preparation and serving of meals or fundraising. In that service activity, students have the opportunity to interact with the homeless, hear their stories, and come to a richer understanding of their own lives and the lives of this group of strangers. It is often the case that such service deeply transforms these students in incredibly valuable ways. Rarely, however, does that inward orientation manifest itself in an outward orientation of action aimed at actually changing the institutional structures that cause homelessness, or that prevent the homeless from escaping their plight.

This lack of an outward orientation toward acting indicates a classic problem in educational practice: the disconnection between theory (critical theory) and practice (critical pedagogy). I hope to make the case that the basic conceptual structure I have suggested in earlier chapters is its strongest when both the inward and outward come together via rugged individuals acting communally to change institutional structures in the name of social justice. In the end, the distinction between weaker and stronger conceptions of CSL is in the degree to which CSL projects focus on both inward self-reconstruction relative to the outward *and* the degree to which that self-reconstruction is carried over and into acting to reconstruct, to transform, community.

Strong CSL: Getting Some Help from Contemporary Critical Theory

Before rummaging through the contemporary critical theorists' closet, so to speak, for some guidance in constructing a strong version of CSL, I want to comment quickly on my choice of names. I use the distinguishing terms "weak" and "strong," rather than "critical" and "traditional" for several reasons. First, given what I have suggested in terms of its philosophical structure, even in its weakest versions, CSL is inherently critical. CSL is simply nonexistent sans the critically reflective piece that I and others have suggested. Calling CSL critical or traditional has little to no distinguishing meaning, particularly in light of its historic connection to pragmatism, a vehemently critical philosophical perspective.

Second, the term critical, so in vogue these days (along with the very annoying prefix "post-" continually placed in front of an "ism" of some kind or other), has gathered some unfortunate though political baggage over years. It is increasingly associated with a particular political orientation toward the far left (as has, unfortunately, the concept of social justice—an issue I deal with later in this chapter). I hope to avoid that orientation as much as possible, and attempt, in my naming it strong, to move CSL toward a more neutral space within democracy, being ever mindful that complete objectivity is impossible and probably undesirable.

Third, and as I mentioned earlier, I have a bit of a love/hate relationship with critical theory and pedagogy so named. In the end, what critical theorists do is simply good pragmatic analysis, reflective of the pragmatic tradition—critical theory seeks to examine concepts as they operate in lived experience, albeit in some rather mystical kinds of language. I do, however, think that critical theory and critical pedagogy aid us in seeing a bit more clearly the internal/external nexus wherein oppressive systemic structures might be met and defeated, particularly when the critical linguistic veil is lifted just a bit. What follows, then, is a very simple, necessarily underdeveloped, synopsis of what critical theorists generally rely on to critique social and educational practice done with an eye toward developing a strong conception of CSL.

The Value of Theory

Like Amy Gutmann and John Dewey, critical theorists rely heavily on...well, theory. Sound theory provides the framework to investigate experiences from a particular standpoint. For Dewey as it relates to experiential learning, it was initially essential to have a theory of experience; for Gutmann in her analysis of educational practice in a democracy, it was essential to first theorize the nature of democratic education as the means to construct and critique it. This project has itself been an attempt to theorize CSL as the means to viably reconstruct its practice.

Critical theorists agree on the value of theory, and though they certainly don't agree on a single ultimate theoretical perspective, for the most part they operate on the understanding that human beings are somewhat trapped in the interaction of self and generalized other, of the individual in interaction with cultural, social, sexual, and economic (to list a few) institutional/cultural structures. There are numerous contradictions in that interaction of the inward and the outward, including the idea that none of us is completely free (an idea that flows from the notion of community that I outlined in Chapter Five). This theoretical perspective provides a critical invitation: engage these self/social contradictions, and in that engagement come to new and better ways of understanding human experience and ways of then acting on those new understandings.

To flesh this out a bit, I return to the CSL project example above: what inward/outward contradictions might be discovered in learning firsthand about the plight of the growing number of homeless people in this country? Several immediately come to mind: the simple contradiction of you and me living in the same place but finding ourselves in nearly inconceivably different spaces; the contradiction of hard-working people finding themselves suddenly homeless; and the glaring contradiction that we live in the wealthiest nation in history, while so many of our citizens sleep on our streets. In these contradictions come pedagogically valuable, teachable moments that lend themselves to a deeper self-understanding and, when CSL is at its strongest, to the potential for communally acting against the structures that support or cause homelessness.

The Social Construction of Knowledge

A second underlying theme of critical theory—and therefore, critical pedagogy—is that important kinds of knowledge, personal and public, are "constructed" in the social interaction of self and others, as well as self and culture. As such, the more important ways of knowing are not those that are merely technical or practical, meaning those that can be verified in the physical testing of them, or those forms of knowledge that can liberate an individual (as in classical liberalism discussed in Chapter Five). For critical theorists/pedagogues, again, the focus is on the interaction, or the contradictions in these two types of knowledge; a contradiction that often leads to critiquing institutionally oppressive structures in need of restructuring.

Our serving-food-to-the-homeless project is a nice example. There certainly are technical lessons to be learned in, for example, preparing and serving the food; or in documenting the number and type of homeless in a community; or helping to plan the food pantry's budget, or in fundraising. There is also something to learn about such notions as individual responsibility, capitalism, the traditional American work ethic, and the liberating idea that one supposedly "can pull himself up with his own boot straps."

Critical pedagogy is, however, much more interested in constructing knowledge that is akin to Habermas' "emancipatory" knowledge. That is, in the contradictions found within the physical facts of homelessness and the fact that most homeless folks would be just as happy to pull themselves up with their own bootstraps, if they only had bootstraps, is the knowledge that the fact of homelessness is, at least in part, due to institutionalized knowledge and practices that oppress. A strong CSL project would be interested in, again, transformationally changed individuals rugged enough to organize communal action toward ending or reducing the sway of such oppressive knowledge thereby transforming community. The emancipatory knowledge found in these contradictions is meant to not only liberate particular classes of people, but to liberate all people—we are all, in different ways and to differing degrees, oppressed. The outward acting, however, can only happen when inward habits of the heart are examined, rediscovered, or rebuilt, in the interaction with the outer and the other.

Hegemony

Of all the mystical terminology in critical theory and critical pedagogy, I think hegemony is perhaps its most important contribution to educational theory, and social/political theory more generally. The idea that humans work in the milieu of self/other, self/culture, and self/institutional structures, and that there are important contradictions in those interactions, was said and/or implied by others long before critical theorists came along; and the same is true of the idea that knowledge is socially constructed. However, the nexus that hegemony points us toward is, I believe, quite important.

Peter McLaren writes that hegemony

> refers to the maintenance of domination not by the sheer exercise of force but primarily through consensual social practices, social forms, and social structures produced in specific sites such as the church, the state, the school, the mass media, the political system, and the family. By social practices, I refer to what people do and say.[4]

As such, hegemony directs us back to the understanding of the grown-up version of liberalism I suggested in Chapter Five.

The notion of hegemony points out a bit of a Jedi mind trick that both classical liberals and classical communitarians play on themselves. The freedom-from liberal believes that individuals are somehow free from covert restrictions of freedom so long as there are no overt restrictions; the communitarian convinces herself that community institutional structures, moral and otherwise, are the means to achievement only, not the source of oppression or restriction. Neither wants to admit that "consensual social practices" can oppress. Hegemony, in its suggestion that we are complicit in our own oppression, asks that we look closely at how communal structures work, with an eye to reconstructing them toward an ever-increasing form of emancipatory knowledge. I think that project begins in the grown-up version of liberalism laid out in Chapter Five and can be completed with the addition of the hegemonic perspective.

Without this understanding of hegemony, our feeding the homeless project can very quickly turn into a miseducative experience where existing oppressive structures and hegemonic personal worldviews are further entrenched, rather than actively examined, increasingly understood, and reasonably reconstructed. The student, whether coming from the classical liberal or classical communitarian perspective (or someplace in between), might quickly and easily conclude that the homeless are homeless because of a character flaw that is within the individual's complete control—if they would just muster up the gumption to fix themselves.

Hegemony, on the other hand, points us to the much more complicated interactive self/social structures that allow dominant ideologies to oppress all of us as well as whole classes of people— again, remember our historic and various ongoing civil-rights movements. The American mythology is a perfect example of an oppressive dominant ideology: if someone cannot achieve success (most often conceived of in economic terms), it is solely the fault of the individual, not society or existing oppressive structures. This allows us to ignore many social problems because they are not really social problems at all.[5]

For CSL to meet its strong potential, teachers must carefully guide students to the understanding that things usually are not as simple as they seem. In so doing, the inward reconstruction of worldviews and a rugged orientation toward restructuring the institutional causes of homelessness (or any other individually/communally felt social problem) can be honed and further developed—emancipatory knowledge can be constructed—the inward and outward interact to create individual and communal agents of change who then are available to institute actual change in lived experience.

Ideology and Social Reproduction

At the risk of beating the proverbial dead horse (as the themes begin to repeat themselves), I will briefly take up the critical perspective on ideology and social reproduction, and simply note that they reveal further structural understandings that critical theorists/pedagogues typically take into account. These other notions include such issues as social class, culture (dominant, subordinate, and sub-), the hidden curriculum, aesthetics, economics, typically Freudian conceptions of self, and so forth. Importantly, ideology and social reproduction point us to the cause and result of our own complicity in our own oppression.

Ideology, for critical theorists, typically and rather simply means a way of *viewing* the world that leads to ways of *acting* in the world through social practices that we accept as commonsensical. I have elsewhere suggested that ideology is akin to Stephen Pepper's notion of the root metaphor—a metaphorical worldview that directs us to only act in ways suggested by that root metaphor.[6] When that metaphorical understanding goes unquestioned, it develops into a Deweyan "belief" that restricts possible conceptions of what constitutes the good life. Ironically enough, social reproduction, particularly in the workings of the dominant American ideology, develops out of classical liberalism— an irony, as noted in an earlier chapter, that John Dewey pointed out.

Social reproduction entails the idea that existing institutional structures, structures created from and by the culturally dominant ideology and its adherents, work to reproduce existing social/economic/ethnic/gender class divisions such that the dominant social/economic/ethnic classes remain dominant, marginalized social/economic/ethnic/gender classes remain marginalized, and oppressed social/economic/ethnic classes remain oppressed (one could certainly add religious, linguistic, and other classes to the list).

In examining our CSL project of caring for the homeless, these conceptions point us toward an outward-in orientation, rather than an inward-out orientation as previous critical conceptions have suggested. In examining our own actions, we can see the impact dominant ideology has on us, and in that examination is the opportunity to restructure our root metaphors such that habitual, somewhat unquestioned habits of acting in the world might be adjusted and made more conscious—a process Freire called "conscientization."[7]

In the self-awareness of our acting, in this case toward the people who are homeless and in reaction to their stories of homelessness, we might shift our ideologies, and in so doing, shift our "actings" in the world. Again, in a strong CSL project it is incumbent upon the teacher to guide this reflective work in meaningful ways such that the felt-difficulty is personally meaningful to the student and results in growth relative to both inner reconstruction of habits, and outer modes of acting.

From this point, I leave it to the reader to further peruse the work of the critical theorists. Before I make some final concluding comments regarding the possible nature of strong CSL, however, there is one more contentious issue that needs addressing: social justice as an inward/outward habit and overarching aim of strong CSL.

Strong CSL and "Social Justice"

The reticence among my students when I ask them to read more contemporary critical theory is not only about the rather mystical quality of its language; it is also a reticence (and sometimes a vehement resistance), as I mentioned above, resulting from the sometimes dogmatic political baggage it has gathered around itself over the years. I am sympathetic to that concern. Sometimes critical theorists, as we all do at times, forget that it is dogmatism (of any kind) that makes us so complicit in our own intellectual, social, economic, and political oppression.[8]

Unfortunately, the notion of social justice has also gathered up some political baggage of its own over the years, or more accurately, has had that baggage put on its back by folks from an equally dogmatic perspective, one informed by radical classical liberalism and most often called the conservative right. The status of social justice is an essential concern particularly for the construction of strong CSL as CSL has a natural inclination toward acting for and in the service of social justice; in fact, social justice is an increasingly inherent means and end entailed in increasingly stronger

CSL practice. This, of course, begs a philosophically important
question: how should social justice be conceived of within the particular practice of CSL and educational practice generally? There
is some recent history here.

The political suspicion of social-justice education/educators
from the political right was most clearly seen in a battle several
years ago over the National Council for Accrediting Teacher Education's (NCATE) removal of "social justice" from its list of desired
teacher dispositions. The removal of social justice came as part of
the Council's reauthorization in 2006 as the national accrediting
body of teacher education programs; and its removal came at the
behest of traditionally right-wing political organizations who suggested that social justice, as a "radical social agenda," promoted
"political ideology in the education of teachers"[9] Battling the perception that, like some critical theorists, social-justice educators
begin with some politically and socially dogmatic worldviews—
worldviews described by the right as liberal, radical, Marxist,
etc.—is ongoing and is a bit troubling given that our history as a
democracy is distinctly oriented toward social justice in its embrace of equality.

What I want to suggest here in response to this charge, is that
social justice, particularly in strong versions of CSL, certainly
cannot be perceived and practiced as an indoctrinating political
project, and, in fact, will not be when social justice is seen in light
of the inward/outward interaction that is its essential hallmark.
To get at that understanding, I rely on some insights from my colleague Jessica Heybach.

In Heybach's piece, "Rescuing Social Justice in Education: A
Critique of the NCATE Controversy," she ponders our present
question: "How might we conceptualize social justice so as to avoid
its reduction to political indoctrination?"[10] In short, her answer to
the social-justice conundrum is found in the same interactive place
that I use to judge the relative strength or weakness of CSL
projects: in the interaction of the "psyche" and the "city" as "inter-
dependent."[11]

Relying on Maxine Green's idea of "wide awakeness," Heybach
argues that social justice is not a form of political indoctrination in
becsause it is initially concerned with the self-reconstructive
process that comes in understanding one's "situatedness" relative
to self and community, psyche and city. So conceived, social justice

is reflective of community, service, and reflective learning as I have outlined them in earlier chapters here; and so conceived, social justice is a characteristic of the historic American rugged individual who acts not on political indoctrination, but on the understanding of how she is situated within the city as exemplified in "the most democratic movements in U.S. history...such as the abolitionist movement, the suffragette movement, and the civil rights movement."[12] And, so conceived, social justice does not necessarily entail outward acting on the part of any particular group, nor even any particular political ideology, since action comes out of the reconstructed self, and that action could quite conceivably go in any social/political direction. In that way, social justice, and CSL with a social-justice aim, is a deeply democratic mode of being, rather than an orientation based on political dogma, radically left, or otherwise.

Implications for Weak and Strong CSL

The implications of the foregoing for growing relatively stronger CSL projects is found in the degree of intensity such projects encourage in the inward/outward construction of self and community. CSL projects that encourage the informed deliberative democratic activity described in the previous chapter, projects that aim to ease symptoms rather than fix communally felt problems, can certainly be weakly successful; however, CSL projects that work to affect inward democratic habits of the heart; projects that encourage a nonrepressive, nondiscriminatory analysis of our situatedness within historic and contemporary systemic modes of oppression; projects whose goal is both self-reconstruction and community transformation via solving communally felt problems; projects that begin in the felt problems of individuals-turned-communal and that encourage the development of rugged individualism as manifested in the work of such people as Martin Luther King, Jr. are ever-increasingly stronger. This relative strength grows as service, experiential learning, and critical reflection are incorporated in school practice out and into the broader community, thereby growing and supporting a sense of community in its grown-up liberal understanding. In so doing, strong CSL projects can help schools to "build a new social order." And in so doing, they are deeply educational—and certainly dangerous, particularly to dominating and dominant ideologies and ideologues who have a vested interest in further institutional oppression.

CHAPTER ELEVEN

A Critique of Practice

Introduction

At the outset of this project, I committed to keeping the discussion relevant and practical and though each of the preceding chapters has provided some "implications for practice," admittedly, these suggestions have been somewhat vague. As a way to bring more particular relevance to the conceptual structure I have suggested, I will conclude by examining more closely an actual CSL project: the CSL PARKnership project described in Chapter One. In so doing, I attempt to show how the project I was involved in could have—in fact should have—worked in reference to both the weak and the increasingly strong conceptions I have outlined here.

Rather than look at all three projects, I will look at one of them: the production of the video tour/documentary of Ravine State Gardens in Palatka, Florida. The other two projects suffered the same fate as the video project, caused by the same kinds of conceptual mistakes, and so there is no need to go beyond that project to see the relevance of a sound conceptual basis for any CSL project. In the critique I will also make suggestions that P–12 teachers might adopt and mold to fit their own school community, from both weak and strong perspectives, and through the lenses of community, service, experiential learning, and reflection.

The PARKnership Video Project

Before describing how the project process went, I want to admit up front that all three of the projects were doomed to fail from the outset. None of the three met the requirements of even the weakest form of CSL for one simple reason: they were not developed by the students based on their felt difficulties, individually or communally, and therefore, were not sourced in the developed interests of those who would carry out the projects, nor even those who were to be served. As I explained in Chapter One, I simply sat down with several park rangers, pen and grant requirements in hand, and let them tell me what the park needed. As such, it failed on all counts. The first and most essential practical requirement is that projects be of interest to and related to truly felt problems on the part of students and those community members *with* whom the work should have been carried out, and who should be essentially involved from its very impetus.

So, how did we decide on a video project? The core problem that the park personnel wanted to solve was that of declining attendance. For several years their attendance numbers had been dropping, and they were itching for the development of some attractive additions that would draw more people to the park. Of special interest to the park (and parks statewide) was increasing the numbers of both the elderly and the physically/emotionally needy (I apologize for not knowing the current politically correct turn of phrase for either of these groups—it is difficult to keep up with the "PC" crowd.)

Ravine State Gardens was and is an especially difficult nut to crack in this regard, as the heart of the park was a rather dangerously winding, navigationally treacherous system of trails that lead deep into a naturally occurring ravine. In considering these issues, we (the park rangers and I) struck upon two solutions: the construction of a railed boardwalk that would allow most park visitors access to the ravine. And for those interested parties who could not, even with a boardwalk, physically navigate the ravines, a video tour of the park that would include a narrative of the history, the flora, and the fauna of the park, to be made available for viewing in the all-purpose meeting room and for purchase. (In case you're curious, the butterfly garden fell into the category of additional attractions that might draw more attendance from people of all walks of life and was located close to its entrance.)

Once the grant funding was secured, I recruited the district media production specialist to instruct us as to the process entailed in producing such a video: (1) Investigate all the aspects of the park we wanted included in the video: its history (Ravine State Gardens was built with Depression-era monies and previously unemployed Depression-era workers in the Civilian Conservation Corps.); its flora (including the increasing number of non-native "invasive" plants that were beginning to appear in the park); and its fauna. (2) Write a narrative based on that research that would then be used as a guide for the actual videotaping, a narrative outline of sorts, to ensure an efficient use of time and resources. (3) Edit the video. (4) Record the narrative over the edited video (steps 3 and 4 being accomplished by groups of students in the district media lab). (5) Produce multiple copies of the video.

Before getting to how this video project could have been at the very least a nominally weak version of CSL, and how it could have become a particularly strong version of it, I want to say something about Mr. Smith (and yes, that really is his name).

As it turns out, the year before these projects were undertaken, the local high school had just become the school home to the most severely disabled students in West Putnam County Florida. With those students came Mr. Smith, whom I can only describe as the St. Theresa of special-needs kids. He was amazing to watch. I had a particularly good vantage point for observing Mr. Smith in his work: my classroom was near the restroom and I was in the habit of hanging out in the cafeteria at lunch, to check on students and generally socialize with them (a valuable practice for any teacher). From what I can tell, he spent every minute of his school day, every day (rarely did he miss a day) with these students, feeding them, cleaning them, joking with them, communicating with them, changing their diapers—it was quite simply inspirational. I ask that you keep this in mind as I discuss my conclusions as to the theoretical and practical degree of weakness and strength that might be entailed in CSL projects.

As I suggested in Chapters Nine and Ten of this study, the relative weakness or strength of a CSL project, conceptually speaking, turns on the degree to which it is, at its minimally weakest, vaguely democratic: encouraging, on some level, informed, reflectively deliberative, nonrepressive, nondiscriminatory communal action that begins to inculcate some democratic "habits of the heart." A CSL project becomes increasingly stronger as its focus turns toward the potential inward/outward transformation that the project holds—an increased orientation of interaction that informs a truly reconstructed inner growth of rugged individuals (psyche) and the degree to which that inward impact then becomes the outward challenging of oppressive systemic structures (the city). Its strength lies in its potential to interactively transform individuals and whole communities and in-so-doing grow a rather virulent strain of democratic activism, and of communal democracy itself.

Community Critique

Remembering that community has two senses, the school as a community itself and the school as part of the community, rather than marked off from it; and remembering my suggestion that developing rugged individuals who feel community problems is best accomplished in the outward/inward interaction of individuals and the "generalized other" that is the community: to what degree did our project meet even the weakest democratic requirements as I have outlined here? In three words, not at all. As to the school as a community, and remembering Mr. Smith, we did not even reflectively deliberate with him or his students, much less invite them (or the various other special-needs students) to participate. The very people who might have benefited from the project work were never consulted—a group of people who were, or should have been, active participants who could have provided us insight as to whether the video project would accomplish anything toward their enjoyment of the park. Had we done so, both groups, the able and the challenged, could have discussed, thought through, and deliberated as to the value (or lack thereof) that the project provided.

As to a stronger version of CSL, the deliberation that should have happened would have provided the opportunity for both groups of students to learn from one another what community institutional structures existed that aided in making all members able to participate democratically; and more importantly, what institutional structures existed that prevented that community participation. Given a stronger version of CSL, this kind of interaction could very well have lead to solving not just the relatively unimportant park problem, but broader, more essential, community problems of access. In that, truly rugged individuals were certainly never developed, and, of course, no broad community concern with the plight of the disabled was engendered in the students of either group. In fact, I suspect that excluding the very students the project most impacted simply re-entrenched the idea that the disabled are "helpless" and can never provide the insight that they most certainly can provide.

Second, and related to the school as part of the broader community, we did not consult the second population we suspected we were going to help: the elderly. Had we consulted the elderly of the community, even in a weak version, we would have furthered the democratic deliberative ethic, gained insight into what might most help them; and in a stronger version, once again, understood much more deeply those institutionally sourced struggles that our elderly unfortunately had and have. In reflectively deliberating with older community members, we certainly could have gone a long way toward breaking down the stereotypes that the young have of the old, and that the old have of the young. We did neither.

Service

Similarly, given the democratic weakness of the project, the service ethic itself was one of oppression rather than liberation. I suspect that of the oppressive models I outlined in Chapter Five, our service was charity at best, and a form of noblesse oblige at worst. Given that there was no deep and abiding interaction of self with stranger, on the part of either group, the disabled or the elderly, there was no transformation of selves or the community. In fact, once again, this oppressive form of service did precisely the opposite of what it should have: it reinforced stereotypes of served and server—that one group has needs, and the other goods. Imagine the insights that could have been fomented had there been such deep and abiding interaction.

Each of the mistakes we made with the CSL components above, community and service, points to a very important practical suggestion: CSL projects should, in either version, incorporate as many actors as is possible, from both within the school community and from without. Most essentially, CSL instructors must create the space required for the server/served, done/done to dialogue to occur and honor that dialogue in acting to solve the felt difficulty on which the project is based. Only in this can projects succeed in its weakest forms and only in this is the hope for increasingly stronger project outcomes.

Learning

I suppose that of all the areas of concern outlined here, the academic component was at least not antithetical to the idea of experiential learning itself. Students did take classroom academics out into the community and use them to create new community resources. In making the video, for example, students wrote, learned videotaping and editing techniques, and came to some understanding of the process of creating a documentary film. However, this too was a missed opportunity.

I mentioned above that Ravine State Gardens was built during the Depression by the Depression-era CCC. At its weakest democratic level, that project might have turned into a rather poignant study of the era, including the causes and results of the great Depression; the causes and results of World War II; the plight of American citizens caught in the throes of the worst economic period in our history. At its strongest, it should have been the opportunity to study the Depression in light of current issues: economic inequality, the current recession, the politics of economic oppression, the history of the Federal Reserve, contemporary poverty, the system of capitalism itself. In short, it was an opportunity to go beyond the technical knowledge of "how to," toward the emancipatory knowledge of who I am in contemporary capitalism and what might be done to create a more just system, one that serves all equally. And, of course, there was a missed opportunity to learn about the struggles of two of our marginalized populations, the physically/emotionally disadvantaged and the elderly.

Reflection

Finally, there is the overarching aim of critical reflection, an aim initially missed in that the projects themselves were not sourced in an authentic felt problem on the part of the students. The students did not engage with community members, in or out of the school, and so reflective deliberation never happened. In fact, there was no criticality experienced or engaged in, even at the most basic level: the park rangers and I decided on how to solve the park's perceived problems. And, certainly in a stronger version, no reflection on oppressive institutional structures was even ever mentioned, much less thought through. Solutions were not those of the students and so testing those solutions never happened. Once again, here was a missed opportunity to engage, reflect, create, and test the ideas of students in problems truly felt by students.

The practical ramifications of this missed opportunity are quite simple: CSL instructors must abdicate a good portion of their power and influence. All too often adults underestimated the insight and energy of our young people. In our handing the reins over to

students, we allow them to try out their ideas, to fail and to succeed and these are essential aspects of CSL projects and student
learning.

In the end, this CSL PARKnership project was one of missed
opportunity, a miseducative experience for all involved.

Concluding Thoughts

I leave it to the reader to envision further the myriad possibilities that CSL projects such as this could have entailed. Another of
my father's favorite quotes comes to mind: "the road to hell is
paved with good intentions." Certainly this project (and, I assume,
all CSL projects) had good intentions; but, sans the conceptual understanding such as that provided here, CSL based on good intentions alone will never meet even the weakest democratic aims,
much less the stronger goals of social-justice. I believe that what I
have outlined in these chapters, when put into practice, can make
the CSL story better. I hope you agree. And so I leave you with a
quote from George Counts that nicely sums up both the danger
and the possibilities that a strong version of CSL provides, if we
only remain diligent in vehemently thinking through and applying
its conceptual underpinnings:

> The educational problem is not wholly intellectual in nature. Our
> Progressive schools therefore cannot rest content with giving children an
> opportunity to study contemporary society in all of its aspects. This of
> course must be done, but I am convinced that they should go much farth-
> er. If the schools are to be really effective, they must become centers for
> the building, and not merely for the contemplation, of our civilization.
> This does not mean that we should endeavor to promote particular re-
> forms through the educational system. We should, however, give to our
> children a vision of the possibilities which lie ahead and endeavor to enl-
> ist their loyalties and enthusiasms in the realization of the vision. Also
> our social institutions and practices, all of them, should be critically ex-
> amined in the light of such a vision.[1]

APPENDIX

Selected Research on CSL Outcomes

(by category, chronologically ordered, necessarily abridged)

Academics

Vivian Houser, "Effects of Student-Aide Experience on Tutors' Self-Concept and Reading Skills"(PhD diss., Brigham Young University, 1974).

James Lewis, "What Is Learned in Expository Learning and Learning by Doing?" (PhD diss., University of Minnesota, 1977).

Diane Hedin, "Students as Teachers: A Tool for Improving School Climate and Productivity," *Social Policy* 17 (3) (1987): 42–47.

Stephen Hamilton and R. Shepherd Zelden, "Learning Civics in Community," *Curriculum Inquiry* 17 (1987): 407–420.

Greg Markus, et al. "Integrating Community Service and Classroom Instruction Enhances Learning: Results from an Experiment," *Educational Evaluation and Policy Analysis* 15, no. 4 (1993): 410–419.

Florida Learn & Serve, Florida Learn & Serve 1995–1996 Outcome Data (Tallahassee, FL: Florida State University, 1997).

Alexander W. Astin, Lori J. Vogelgesang, Elaine K. Ikeda, and Jennifer A. Yee, "How Service Learning Affects Students" (Los Angeles, CA: University of California Los Angeles, 2000).

J. Mayhew & Welch, M. A call to service: Service learning as pedagogy in special education programs. *Teacher Education and Special Education, 24*(3), (2001): 208-219.

M. S. Ammon, Furco, A., Chi, B., & Middaugh, E. *Service-learning in California: A profile of the CalServe service-learning partnerships, 1997–2000.* (Berkeley, CA: University of California, Service-Learning Research and Development Center, 2001).

Janet Eyler, Dwight E. Giles Jr., Christine M. Stenson, and Charlene J. Gray, *At a Glance: What We Know about the Effects of Service-Learning on College Students, Faculty, Institutions and Communities, 1993–2000*, 3rd ed. (Nashville, TN: Vanderbilt University, 2001).

Shelley H. Billig & Meyer, S. (2002). *Evaluation of the Hawaiian Studies Program at Waianae High School for CREDE.* Denver, CO: RMC Research Corporation.

M.M. Klute. *Antioch's Community-Based School Environmental Education (CO-SEED): Quantitative evaluation report.* Denver, CO: RMC Research Corporation (December, 2002).

Shelley H. Billig, & Klute, M. M. (2003, April). *The impact of service-learning on MEAP: A large-scale study of Michigan Learn and Serve grantees.* Presentation at National Service-Learning Conference, Minneapolis, MN (April 2003)

Susan Root, et al., eds, *Improving Service-Learning Practice: Research on Models to Enhance Impacts.* Charlotte, NC: New Age Publishing, 2005.

Karen McKnight Casey, et al. *Advancing Knowledge in Service-Learning Research to Transform the Field* (Charlotte: Information Age Publishing, 2006)

Character/Civic Education

Greg Markus, Jeffery Howard and D.C. King, "Integrating Community Service and Classroom Instruction Enhances Learning: Results from an Experiment," *Educational Evaluation and Policy Analysis* 15, no. 4 (1993): 410–419.

Richard Battistoni, "Service Learning and Democratic Citizenship." *Theory into Practice* 36, no. 3 (summer 1997): 142–154.

Alexander W. Astin and Lori J. Sax, "How Undergraduates Are Affected by Service Participation," *Journal of College Student Development* 39 (1998): 251–263.

Stanley Johnson and Markus Bozeman, "Service Learning and the Development of Social Responsibility" (Paper presented at the Annual Convention of the Central States Communication Association, Chicago, IL, 1998).

Arnold Stukas, Marianne Snyder, and Eric Clary, "The Effects of 'Mandatory Volunteerism' on Intentions to Volunteer," *Psychological Science* 10 (1998): 59–64.

Alexander W. Astin and Lori J. Sax, "How Undergraduates are Affected by Service Participation," *Journal of College Student Development* 39 (1998): 251–263.

Alexander W. Astin, Lori J. Sax and John Avalos, "Long-Term Effects of Volunteerism during the Undergraduate Years," *Review of Higher Education* 22 (1999): 187–202.

Janet Eyler and Dwight Giles Jr., *Where's the Learning in Service-Learning?* (San Francisco, CA: Jossey-Bass, 1999).

Kerry Rockquemore and Regan Schaffer, "Toward a Theory of Engagement: A Cognitive Mapping of Service-Learning Experiences," *Michigan Journal of Community Service Learning* 7 (Fall 2000): 14–25.

Lori Vogelgesang and Alexander W. Astin, "Comparing the Effects of Service-Learning and Community Service" *Michigan Journal of Community Service Learning* 7 (Fall 2000): 25–34.

Bernadette Chi. *Service-Learning as "Citizenship Education": The Promise and the Puzzles.* Washington, DC: Corporation for National Service, 2000.

Robert Rhoads, "Explorations of the Caring Self: Rethinking Student Development and Liberal Learning" (Paper presented at the annual meeting of the American Education Research Association, Chicago, IL, 2000).

Christopher Payne, "Changes in Involvement as Measured by the Community Service Involvement Preference Inventory," *Michigan Journal of Community Service Learning* 7 (Fall 2000): 41–53.

Marylinne Boyle-Baise and James Kilbane, "What Really Happens? A Look Inside Service-Learning for Multicultural Teacher Education," *Michigan Journal of Community Service Learning* 7 (Fall 2000): 54–64.

James Potthoff, et al., "Preparing for Democracy and Diversity: The Impact of a Community-Based Field Experience on Preservice Teachers' Knowledge, Skills, and Attitudes," *Action in Teacher Education* 22 (2000): 79–92.

Robert Rhoads, "Explorations of the Caring Self: Rethinking Student Development and Liberal Learning" (Paper presented at the annual meeting of the American Education Research Association, Chicago, IL, 2000).

Andrew Furco. "Is service-learning really better than community service? A study of high school service." In A. Furco & S. H. Billig (Eds.), *Advances in service-learning research: Vol.1. Service-learning: The essence of the pedagogy* (pp. 23–50). (Greenwich, CT: Information Age Publishers, 2002).

Janet Eyler & Shelley H. Billig, eds. *Deconstructing Service-Learning: Research Exploring Context, Participation, and Impacts* (Charlotte: Information Age Publishing, 2003).

A. Bowden, Shelley H. Billig & Barbara A. Holland. *Scholarship for Sustaining Service-Learning and Civic Engagement* (Charlotte: Information Age Publishing, 2008).

Barbara E. Moely, Shelley H. Billig, Barbara A. Holland. *Creating Our Identities in Service-Learning and Community Engagement* (Charlotte: New Information Age Publishing, 2009).

Community Transformation

M. Duckenfield & L. Swanson. *Service learning: Meeting the needs of youth at risk. A dropout prevention research report.* Clemson, SC: National Dropout Prevention Center (1992).

C.W. Maybach, C. W. (1996). "Investigating urban community needs: Service learning from a social justice perspective." *Education and Urban Society, 28*(2), (1996): 224-236.

B. H. Hobbes, B. H. "Increasing the 4-H participation of youth for high-risk environments." *Journal of Extension, 37*(4). Retrieved from http://www.joe.org/joe/1999august/rb1.php (1999).

D. Kirby. *Emerging answers: Research findings on programs to reduce teen pregnancy.* (Washington, DC: National Campaign to Prevent Teen Pregnancy, 1999).

L. Lantieri. "Hooked on altruism: Developing social responsibility in at-risk youth." *Reclaiming Children and Youth: Journal of Emotional and Behavioral Problems, 8*(2), (1999):83-87.

S. Meyer, & K. Sandel, K. *Research on service-learning and teen pregnancy and risk behavior prevention: Bibliography.* (Denver, CO: RMC Research Corporation, 2001).

NOTES

Preface

1 Weber, *The Protestant Ethic,* 182.
2 West, *Democracy Matters,* 177.
3 Dewey, *Art as Experience,* 199.

Chapter Two
Making the Case for Philosophy

1 A portion of this chapter was previously published in Eric Sheffield, "Beyond Abstraction: Philosophy as a Practical Qualitative Research Method," *The Qualitative Report* 9 (4) (2004): 760-769.
2 Sheffield, "Philosophical (Re)thinking Described and Applied."
3 MacIntyre, *After Virtue,* 187.
4 Ibid., 190.
5 Feuer. "American Philosophy Is Dead," 35.
6 Hocking, *Types of Philosophy,* 3.
7 Ibid., 10.
8 Hook, "Does Philosophy Have a Future?" 52.
9 Titus, "Philosophy and the Contemporary Scene," 24.
10 Giarelli and Chambliss, "Philosophy of Education as Qualitative Inquiry," 33–35.
11 Sherman, Course Handout, 1995.
12 Dewey, *How We Think,* 72.
13 Ibid., 74–75.
14 Sherman, "Philosophy with Guts," 7.
15 Rorty, "Philosophy in America Today," 183–200; Seeskin. "Never Speculate, Never Explain,"19–33.
16 Toulmin, "The Recovery of Practical Philosophy," 337–352.
17 James, *Pragmatism and the Meaning of Truth,* 53.
18 Dewey, *Reconstruction in Philosophy,* 94.
19 Corporation for National Service, www.cns.gov/learn. Accessed 6-26-10.
20 Ibid.
21 Stanton, "Service Learning: Groping toward a Definition," 85.
22 Alliance for Service-Learning in Education Reform www.servicelearning.org/what_ is_service-learning/service-learning_is. Accessed 8-23-10.
23 Giles, Honnet, and Migliore, eds., *Research Agenda for Combining Service and Learning in the 1990s,* 7.
24 Shumer, "Describing Service-Learning: A Delphi Study."

25 The claim I make here, that there is substantial conceptual "muddiness" within in the workings of CSL, is not to suggest that valuable conceptual frameworks have not been constructed around or out of CSL. See, for example, Rhoads' *Community Service and Higher Learning* and Lisman's *Toward a Civil Society*. Also, and as I explain in later chapters, much "philosophical" work in CSL of late has come from the critical theory camp. In each case, I believe such work can be more powerful when a clear conception of the basic constituents of CSL is available for discussion.

Chapter Three
A Brief History of an Educational Idea

1   Dewey, *Experience and Education*, 6–7.
2   Adams and Reynolds, "The Long Conversation: Tracing the Roots of the Past," 21.
3   See Pollock, *Three Decades of Service-Learning in Higher Education (1966–1996)*; Stanton, Giles and Cruz, eds., *Service-learning: Pioneers Reflect on Its Origins, Practice, and Future*. Other brief histories include R Kraft, "Service Learning: An Introduction to Its Theory, Practice, and Effects"; Giles and Eyler, "The Theoretical Roots of Service-learning in John Dewey"; Hepburn, "Service Learning in Civic Education"; Conderman and Patryla. "Service Learning: The Past, Present, and the Promise"; Clark, *Power and Service-Learning: Implications in Service-Learning for Social Justice*. I leave it to the reader to search online for a growing list of historical outlines of CSL. One such example is Ohio State University's institutional recounting of campus CSL endeavors: http://service-learning.osu.edu/history.php, accessed 8-25-10.
4   Kraft, "Service Learning: An Introduction"; Liu, Introduction to *Service-Learning*.
5   Stanton, Giles, and Cruz, *Service-Learning*.
6   O'Connell, "Service–Learning as a Strategy for Innovation in Undergraduate Instruction," 5.
7   Alexis de Tocqueville, *Democracy in America*.
8   Robert Bellah, et al., *Habits of the Heart: Individualism and Commitment in American Life*.
9   Seymour Lipset, Jr., *American Exceptionalism*.
10 Horace Mann, *Twelfth Annual Report Covering the Year 1848*, 90.
11 I am, of course, mindful that the full political and educational participation of minorities, African American and otherwise, remains to this day an important ongoing endeavor.
12 Blackwell, *A Black Institution Pioneering Adult Education: Tuskegee Institute Past and Present*; Schall ed., *Stony the Road: Chapters in the History of Hampton Institute*; (Mary Francis Armstong, *Hampton and Its Students*.
13 Paul Kellogg, foreword to *School Acres: An Adventure in Rural Education*, xiii.
14 William Heard Kilpatrick, *Philosophy of Education*, 243.
15 Cooley and House, *School Acres: An Adventure in Rural Education*, 3.
16 Ibid., 56.

17 Dewey, *Experience and Education,* 67.

18 Dewey, *Democracy and Education,* 329.

19 Kraft, "Service Learning"; Liu, Introduction to *Service-Learning.*

20 James, "The Moral Equivalent of War."

21 Dewey, *The School and Society,* 52.

22 Kilpatrick. *The Project Method,* 12.

23 Ibid., 17.

24 Dewey, *How We Think: A Restatement of the Relation of Reflective Thinking to the Educative Process.*

25 Dewey, *The Way Out of Educational Confusion;* Counts, *Dare the School Build a New Social Order?*

26 Merrill, *Roosevelt's Forest Army.*

27 Kilpatrick, Introduction to *Youth Serves the Community,* 11.

28 Ibid., 14.

29 Hanna, *Youth Serves the Community,* 11.

30 Ibid., 36.

31 Ibid., 40.

32 For an informative discussion of the progressive movement in education and the "soft pedagogy" issue, see Zilversmit, *Changing Schools.*

33 Important to note here is that this was the first substantial federal foray into educational funding and opened the door to the mother of all federal educational interventions, No Child Left Behind, a few decades later.

34 For a discussion of national service and its relationship to CSL, see Eberly, *National Service: A Promise to Keep.*

35 O'Connell, "Service–Learning as a Strategy for Innovation in Undergraduate Instruction," 5.

36 As Eberly points out in *National Service,* these options never materialized.

37 Eberly, *National Service,* 66.

38 ACTION, "High School Student Volunteers," 1.

39 Ibid., 4–5.

40 One such "fringe school" was the New Orleans Free School. See www.educationrevolution.org/nofreeschool.html, accessed 9-13-10.

41 Sigmon, "Service-Learning: Three Principles," 9.

42 Honnet and Poulsen, "Principles of Good Practice for Combining Service and Learning," 1–2.

43 Americorps funds and supports college student service in exchange for some tuition money, and Learn and Serve America provides the same for school- and community-based service-learning projects.

44 These supporters of service learning include such groups as the Association for Experiential Education, Alliance for Service-Learning in Education Reform and universities such as the University of Colorado at Boulder and the University of Michigan.

45 Now called the American Association for Higher Education and Accreditation.

46 McKnight Casey, et al., *Advancing Knowledge in Service-Learning: Research to Transform the Field;* Eyler and Billig eds., *Deconstructing Service Learning: Research Exploring Context, Participation, and Impacts;* Root, Billig, and Callahan, eds., *Improving Service-Learning Practice.*

47 Bringle, Phillips, and Hudson, *The Measure of Service Learning.*
48 Howard, ed., *Michigan Journal of Community Service Learning. Special Issue 2001.*
49 O'Neil, "The Liberal Tradition of Civic Education."
50 Bellah, et al., *Habits of the Heart.*
51 Stanton , "Liberal Arts, Experiential Learning and Public Service," 186.
52 Battistoni, "Service Learning and Democratic Citizenship," 151.
53 Barber, *A Passion for Democracy,* 10.
54 Westheimer and Kahne, "What Kind of Citizen? The Politics of Educating for Democracy," 237-269.
55 Calderón, ed., Introduction to *Race, Poverty, and Social Justice: Multidisciplinary Perspectives through Service Learning.*
56 Johnson and Cope, "Social Justice and Public Policy," 121.
57 Mitchell, "Traditional vs. Critical Service-Learning: Engaging the Literature to Differentiate Two Models," 50.
58 Hill, "Death of a Dream: Service Learning 1994–2010," 2.

Chapter Four
Aims

1 Millard and Bertocci, "Philosophy and Philosophy of Education," 9.
2 If there is any doubt as to the power education has, one need only peruse the history of Hitler's Germany, Stalin's Russia, or even Christian fundamentalism as unveiled in the more recent documentary *Jesus Camp.*
3 Langer, "On the Relations between Philosophy and Education," 141.
4 Perkinson, *The Imperfect Panacea; American Faith in Education, 1865–1965.*
5 Dewey, *Democracy and Education,* 104.
6 Ibid., 105.
7 Kraft, "Service Learning," 17.
8 Putnam, *Bowling Alone: The Collapse and Revival of American Community.*
9 Amy Gutmann explains this at length in *Democratic Education.*
10 "Classroom" here means in an introductory, informational manner rather than in immediate application.
11 Dewey, *Democracy and Education,* 119.
12 Cunningham, "Assessment: An Integral Part of Experience and Learning."
13 Eyler, et.al., *At A Glance: What We Know about the Effects of Service-Learning on College Students, Faculty, Institutions and Communities, 1993–2000,* 3rd ed.
14 For example, "The Wingspread Principles" mentioned in Chapter Two of this study puts engaging "people in responsible and challenging actions for the common good" at the top of its list, and the Commission on National and Community Service also mentioned earlier lists "community needs," "collaboration," and "the development of a sense of caring for others" as necessary goals of service learning.
15 Bernadette Chi explains that service learning is generally founded in one of four conceptions of citizenship: direct democracy, civic republican democracy, liberal democracy, and participatory democracy. Chi, *Service-Learning as "Citizenship Education,"* 9–13.

16 Bellah et al., *Habits of the Heart.*
17 Tocqueville, *Democracy in America*; Lipset, Jr., *American Exceptionalism.*
18 Hanna, *Youth Serves the Community*, 36.
19 Ibid., 36.
20 Ibid., 37.
21 Kilpatrick, Introduction to *Youth Serves the Community*, 11

Chapter Five
Community: A Rose by Any Other Name...

1 Putnam. *Bowling Alone*, 258 ff; Blakely and Snyder, *Fortress America.*
2 Counts, *Dare the School Build a New Social Order?*
3 Berlin, *Four Essays on Liberty*, 121.
4 Ibid., 123.
5 Theobald, *Teaching the Commons*, 61.
6 Ibid., 61.
7 Taylor, *The Ethics of Authenticity*, 37.
8 Etzioni, *Spirit of Community*, 63.
9 MacIntyre, *After Virtue.*
10 Dewey in fact discusses the "individualism" problem of liberalism in a three-lecture series delivered at the University of Virginia and published together as "Liberalism and Social Action," in *John Dewey: The Later Works*, 5–65.
11 Dewey. *Individualism Old and New*, 26.
12 Marcuse, *Eros and Civilization.*
13 Marcuse, *One-Dimensional Man*, 4–6.
14 Thayer-Bacon, "Beyond Liberal Democracy,"19–30; Sheffield, "Root Metaphors, Paradigm Shifts, and Democratically Shared Values," 105–118.
15 I will side with Thayer-Bacon in believing that the community theory I suggest here lends itself to democracy as conceived in Benjamin Barber's strong democracy or Judith Green's deep democracy.
16 Dewey, "Liberalism and Social Action," 31.
17 Ibid., 30.
18 Dewey, *Individualism Old and New*, 42.
19 Mead, *Mind, Self and Society from the Standpoint of a Social Behaviorist*, 154.
20 Ibid., 262.
21 Critical theorists express the concern that "positivism" is part and parcel of the internalizing of dominant ideologies that repress individualism and limit autonomy. It is much the same sentiment as Thayer-Bacon and I express here in more practical terms. See Marcuse, *Essay on Liberation*; Adorno, "Scientific Experiences of a European Scholar in America"; and Kristeva, *Desire in Language.*
22 Thayer-Bacon, "Renascent Liberalism," 28.
23 Kuhn, *The Structure of Scientific Revolutions.*
24 Sheffield, "Root Metaphors, Paradigm Shifts, and Democratically Shared Values," 111.
25 Though, in several places, maybe most convincingly in *Democracy and Education*, Dewey writes that communities are not formed by "living in physical

proximity" but "because they all work for a common end." Dewey, *Democracy and Education*, 4–5.

Chapter Six
Service: Self and Stranger

1   Tocqueville, *Democracy in America*, 197.
2   Bellah et al., *Habits of the Heart*, 38.
3   On the question of our founders and religion, there seems to be much misinformation. As Nel Noddings, among others, points out, our founders were "deists," not fundamentalist Christians and not much like contemporary Christians at all. See Noddings' discussion in *Educating for Intelligent Belief or Unbelief*.
4   Lipset, Jr., *American Exceptionalism*.
5   Radest, *Community Service*.
6   Payton, *Philanthropy*, 47.
7   Ibid., 118–130.
8   Ibid., 52–53.
9   O'Connell, *Philanthropy in Action*, vii.
10 Interestingly , John Dewey suggested that the "parasitic dependence" on "the public dole" has an "ironical sound," given that those same classically liberal-oriented commentators who lament the situation continue to control and limit access by the suffering masses via the same liberally oriented contention toward the individual. "Liberalism and Social Action," in *John Dewey: The Later Works*, 29.
11 Radest, *Community Service*; Barber, *An Aristocracy of Everyone: The Politics of Education and the Future of America*; Rhoads, *Community Service and Higher Learning*.
12 Noddings, *Caring*, 30.
13 Dewey, *How We Think*.
14 Barber, *Aristocracy of Everyone*, 207.
15 Coles, *The Call of Service*, 54.
16 Ibid.
17 Ibid.
18 Barber, *Aristocracy of Everyone*, 210.
19 Coles discusses this at length, particularly through relating his conversations with Anna Freud on this topic. See particularly, Coles, *The Call of Service*.
20 Buckley, "National Debt, National Service," *New York Times*, October 18, 1990.
21 Radest, *Community Service*, 44.
22 Radest, *Community Service*; Wade, *Community Service Learning*; Rhoads, *Community Service and Higher Learning*; Liu, Introduction to *Service-Learning*.
23 Radest. *Community Service*, 79.
24 Rhoads, *Community Service and Higher Learning*, 138.
25 Kendall, "Combining Service and Learning: an Introduction," 19.
26 Noddings, *Caring*, 30.
27 Radest, *Community Service*,179–180.

28 Ibid.,180.
29 Dewey, *How We Think*.
30 Kraft, "Service Learning," 11.
31 Dewey, *Experience and Education*, 13–14.
32 Ibid., 183
33 Radest is clear about his indebtedness to Rorty on the discussion of solidarity, but equally as clear in his distancing himself from Rorty's radical pluralism. Radest, *Community Service*, 183. See Rorty, *Contingency, Irony, and Solidarity*.
34 Radest, *Community Service*, 183.
35 James, *Psychology: The Briefer Course*, 17.
36 Dewey, *Experience and Education*, 89–90.
37 Radest, *Community Service*, 184.
38 Rorty, *Contingency, Irony, and Solidarity*, 87.
39 Noddings, *Caring*, 30.
40 Radest, *Community Service*, 185.
41 It would be a mistake not to reference the work of George Herbert Mead here. Mead was the first to argue that selves can only develop in the "me-other" relationship taken into account by the concept of solidarity. See Mead, *Mind, Self, and Society*.
42 Tocqueville, *Democracy in America*; Lipset Jr., *American Exceptionalism*.
43 Radest, *Community Service*, 185.
44 Dewey, *Experience and Education*, 10.
45 Radest, *Community Service*, 188.
46 Radest, *Community Service*, 177.
47 Ibid., 188.
48 Dewey, *How We Think*, 15.
49 Dewey, *Experience and Education*, 33–36.
50 Dewey, *Lectures in the Philosophy of Education 1899*, 80.
51 Noddings, *Caring*, 30.
52 Radest, *Community Service*, 185.
53 Dewey, *Experience and Education*, 13–14.
54 For example, Tracy Kidder, *Old Friends*.
55 Putnam, *Bowling Alone*.
56 Ibid., 65–68; C. Lisman, *Toward A Civil Society*; Robert Bellah, et al., *Habits of the Heart*, 39.
57 Radest. *Community Service*; Bellah, et al., *Habits of the Heart*; Lisman, *Toward a Civil Society*; Kendall, *Combining Service and Learning*; Noddings, *Caring*; Rhoads, *Community Service and Higher Learning*.

Chapter Seven
Epistemology

1 See the Corporation for National & Community Service website (www.nationalservice.gov); Stanton, "Service Learning: Groping toward A Definition," 85; and "Standards of Quality for School-based Service Learning."
2 Dewey, *Experience and Education*, 6.

3 Other experiential education practices include wilderness education, adventure education, internships, and animated learning.

4 Dewey, *Experience and Education*, 1.

5 For a discussion of the "either-or" development of epistemological theory as seen at the time of the progressive movement, see Coursault, *The Learning Process*.

6 Dewey, *Experience and Education*, 2.

7 Ibid.

8 Ibid., 3.

9 Howard, "Academic Service Learning," 23.

10 Freire, *Pedagogy of the Oppressed*, 77.

11 Dewey, *Reconstruction in Philosophy*, 31–33;Bacon, *Advancement of Learning*.

12 Kant, *Critique of Pure Reason*.

13 James, *Essays in Pragmatism*144–145.

14 Donaldson and Vinson, "William James, Philosophical Father of Experience-Based Education," 7–8.

15 Ibid., 8.

16 Harkavy and Benson, "De-Platonizing and Democratizing Education as the Bases of Service Learning," 11.

17 Giles and Eyler, "The Theoretical Roots of Service-Learning in John Dewey"; Hepburn, "Service Learning in Civic Education," 136–142.

18 Dewey, *Experience and Education*, 7.

19 Hopkins, *Narrative Schooling*, 6.

20 Dewey, *Democracy and Education*, 3.

21 Dewey, *Democracy and Education*, 9.

22 Ibid., 11.

23 Dewey, *Experience and Education*, 25–26.

24 Ibid., 42. Dewey's emphasis.

25 Dewey, *Democracy and Education*, 52.

26 Dewey, *Experience and Education*, 24.

27 Ibid., 44–45; Dewey, *Democracy and Education*, 17–30.

28 Kilpatrick, *The Project Method*, 4.

29 Ibid., 5.

30 Dewey, *Experience and Education*, 42.

31 Hanna. *Youth Serves the Community*, 35–36.

32 Hesser, "Outcomes Attributed to Service-Learning and Evidence of Changes in Faculty Attitudes about Experiential Education"; Fry and Kolb,"Experiential Learning Theory and Learning Experiences in Liberal Arts Education"; Henderson and Hyre, "Contract Learning"; Doherty, Mentkowski, and Conrad, "Toward a Theory of Undergraduate Experiential Learning," 23.

33 Kolb, *Experiential Learning*, 5.

34 Ibid., 38.

35 Ibid., 38.

36 Ibid., 49.

37 Dewey, *How We Think*, 4–5.

38 Kolb, *Experiential Education*, 41.

39   This "reflective" process will be fully explained in the next chapter.
40   Moore, "Experiential Education as Critical Discourse," 278.
41   Ibid.

Chapter Eight
Reflection: Binding Together Community, Service, and Learning

1   Eyler, "Creating Your Reflection Map," 35.
2   Chickering, *Experience and Learning: An Introduction to Experiential Learning*, 12–18; Mintz and Hesser, "Principles of Good Practice in Service-Learning;" Honnet and Poulsen, *Principles of Good Practice in Combining Service and Learning*.
3   Eyler, Gilesand Schmiede, *A Practitioner's Guide to Reflection in Service-Learning*, 14.
4   Eyler, "Creating Your Reflection Map," 35; Duley, "Field Experience Education"; Boud, Keogh, and Walker, "What Is Reflection in Learning?"; Eyler, Giles, and Schmiede, *A Practitioner's Guide to Reflection in Service-Learning*; Toole and Toole, "Reflection as a Tool for Turning Service Experiences into Learning Experiences"; Maybach. *Second-Year Evaluation of Three Components of Colorado Campus Compact.*
5   Eyler, "Creating Your Reflection Map," 35.
6   Maybach, *Second-Year Evaluation.*
7   Boud, Keogh, and Walker, "Promoting Reflection," 8.
8   Eyler, Giles, & Schmiede, *Practitioner's Guide*, 14.
9   Whitaker, *Managing to Learn*, 3.
10 Eyler, Giles, and Schmiede, *Practitioner's Guide*, 20.
11 Boud, Keogh, and Walker, "Promoting Reflection," 11.
12 Boud, Keogh, and Walker, "Promoting Reflection," 11–12. The 1933 reference is to John Dewey, *How We Think: A Restatement of the Relation of Reflective Thinking to the Educative Process.*.
13 Cooper, "Reading, Writing, and Reflection," 52. Again, the 1933 reference is to Dewey, *How We Think: A Restatement*. The 1984 reference is to Kolb, *Experiential Learning*.
14 Boud, Keogh, and Walker, "Promoting Reflection," 14.
15 Cooper, "Reading, Writing, and Reflection," 51–55; Ghaye and Ghaye, *Teaching and Learning through Critical Reflective Practice*, 2; Kolb, *Experiential Learning*, 5; Jack Mezirow and Associates, *Fostering Critical Reflection in Adulthood*, 5–6.
16 James, *Psychology*, 27.
17 Dewey, *How We Think: A Restatement*, 7.
18 Ibid., 5.
19 Dewey, *Democracy and Education*, 153.
20 Fry and Kolb, "Experiential Learning Theory," 79–92.
21 Dewey, *How We Think: A Restatement*, 12.
22 Sherman, "Philosophy with Guts," 7. Sherman's emphasis.
23 Dewey, *How We Think*, 72. Emphasis mine.
24 Dewey, *How We Think: A Restatement*, 106.
25 Dewey, *How We Think: A Restatement*, 16.

26 Dewey, *Democracy and Education*, 152.
27 Dewey, *How We Think: A Restatement*, 114.
28 Eyler, Giles, and Schmiede, *Practitioner's Guide*, 17.
29 Toole and Toole, "Reflection as a Tool," 102.
30 Diana Falk, "Preflection: A Strategy for Enhancing Reflection," 23.
31 Boud, Keogh, and Walker, "Promoting Reflection," 9.
32 Falk, "Preflection," 23.
33 Toole and Toole, *Reflection as a Tool*, 105. Emphasis theirs.
34 Dewey, *Experience and Education*, 71.
35 Boud, Keogh, and Walker, "Promoting Reflection," 11.
36 Dewey, *How We Think*, 72.
37 Boud, Keogh, and Walker, "Promoting Reflection," 11.
38 Eyler, Giles, and Schmiede, *Practitioner's Guide*, 56-59.
39 Silcox, *A How to Guide to Reflection*, 47.
40 Toole and Toole, *Reflection as a Tool*, 104; Kolb, *Experiential Learning*.
41 Toole and Toole, "Reflection as a Tool,"107.
42 Learn and Serve Florida, *2002 Request for Proposals*.
43 Eyler, Giles Jr., and Schmiede, *Practitioner's Guide to Reflection in Service-Learning*; Hiott, Lyday, and Winecoff, *Service Learning Handbook for Teacher Educators and Practitioners*; Kendall, *Combining Service and Learning*; Points of Light Foundation, *Agencies + Schools = Service Learning: A Training Toolbox*.
44 Dewey, *Experience and Education*, 89–91.

Chapter Nine
Democratic Education: Weak Community Service Learning

1   Dewey, *Democracy and Education*, 328.
2   Dewey, *Democracy and Education*, 328.
3   Perkinson, *The Imperfect Panacea*.
4   Lipset Jr., *American Exceptionalism*.
5   Dewey, *Democracy and Education*, 86–87.
6   Ibid., *Democracy and Education*, 87.
7   Ibid., 99.
8   Gutmann, *Democratic Education*, 3–6.
9   James, *Pragmatism*, 53.
10 Gutmann, *Democratic Education*, 5.
11 Dewey, *How We Think*, 17.
12 Gutmann, *Democratic Education*, 11–12.
13 Whitehead, *The Aims of Education and Other Essays*, 1.
14 Ibid.
15 Dewey, *Democracy and Education*, 99.
16 Some have argued, and Gutmann implies agreement, that Dewey's position lacked an understanding of power relationships. Nonrepression and nondiscrimination are clear attempts to incorporate a defense against oppression. For a discussion of Dewey's detractors and a defense of his position on this issue, see Hewitt, *Dewey and Power*.
17 Tocqueville, *Democracy in America*.

18 Gutmann uses the phrase "conscious social reproduction" throughout her book. It connotes reflective, informed and socially active deliberation as explicitly explained here.Gutmann, *Democratic Education*, 14.
19 Gutmann, 44–45. (Emphasis hers.)
20 Gutmann, *Democratic Education*, 45.
21 Hanna, *Youth Serves the Community*.
22 Honnet and Poulsen, "Principles of Good Practice," 1–2.
23 Kraft, "Service Learning: An Introduction," 11.

Chapter Ten
Toward Strong Community Service Learning

1 Butin, Preface to *Service-Learning in Higher Education*, viii.
2 In the case of the above: Bucknell, Swarthmore, University of Pennsylvania, Tufts, and Widener.
3 And, not surprisingly, one that John Dewey made light of in *Experience and Education*, 3.
4 McLaren, *Life in Schools*, 203.
5 A classic educational study of this phenomenon of social reproduction is Jay MacLeod, *Ain't No Makin' It: Aspirations and Attainment in a Low-Income Neighborhood*.
6 Sheffield, *Root Metaphors*.
7 Freire, *Pedagogy of the Oppressed*, 81.
8 See, for example, Peter McLaren's political tirade in his opening section of the fifth edition of *Life in Schools*.
9 Heybach, "Rescuing Social Justice in Education," 235–236.
10 Ibid., 238.
11 Ibid., 240.
12 Ibid., 241.

Chapter Eleven
A Critique of Practice

1 Counts, *Dare the School Build a New Social Order?*, 25.

Bibliography

ACTION. "High School Student Volunteers." Washington, DC: National Center for Service-Learning.

Adams, Albert and Sherrod Reynolds, "The Long Conversation: Tracing the Roots of the Past." *Journal of Experiential Education* Spring (1981): 10–24.

Adorno, Theodor. "Scientific Experiences of a European Scholar in America." In *The Intellectual Migration*, David Flemming and Bradley Bailyn, eds. Cambridge, MA: Harvard University Press, 1969.

Alliance for Service-Learning in Education Reform, www.servicelearning.org/what_is_service-learning/service-learning_is.

Armstong, Mary Francis. *Hampton and Its Students*. New York: G.P. Putnam's Sons, 1875.

Bacon, Francis. *Advancement of Learning*. New York: P.F. Collier and Son, 1901 [1605].

Barber, Benjamin. *An Aristocracy of Everyone: The Politics of Education and the Future of America*. New York: Ballantine Books, 1992.

Barber, Benjamin. *A Passion for Democracy*. Princeton, NJ: Princeton University Press, 1998.

Battistoni, Richard. "Service Learning and Democratic Citizenship." *Theory into Practice* 36, no. 3 (summer 1997): 142–154.

Bellah, Robert N., Richard Madsen, William M. Sullivan, Ann Swidler, and Steven M. Tipton. *Habits of the Heart: Individualism and Commitment in American Life*. Berkeley, CA: University of California Press, 1985.

Berlin, Isaiah. *Four Essays on Liberty*. Oxford: Oxford University Press, 1969.

Blackwell, Velma. *A Black Institution Pioneering Adult Education: Tuskegee Institute Past and Present*. Unpublished dissertation, 1974.

Blakely, Edward J. and Mary Gail Snyder. *Fortress America: Gated Communities in the United States*. Washington, DC: Brookings Institute, 1997.

Boud, David, Rosemary Keogh, and David Walker. "Promoting Reflection in Learning: A Model." In *Boundaries of Adult Learning* by Richard Edwards, Ann Hanson, and Peter Raggatt, eds. London: Routledge, 1996.

Boud, David, Rosemary Keogh, and David Walker."What Is Reflection in Learning?" In *Reflection: Turning Experience into Learning*, David Boud, Rosemary Keogh, and David Walker, eds., 7–17. London: Kogan Page Ltd., 1985.

Bringle, Robert, Mindy Phillips, and Michael Hudson. *The Measure of Service Learning: Research Scales to Assess Student Experiences*. Washington, DC: American Psychological Association, 2003.

Buckley, William F. "National Debt, National Service," *New York Times*, 18 October, 1990.

Butin, Dan. Preface to *Service-Learning in Higher Education: Critical Discussions*. New York: Palgrave Macmillan, 2005.

Calderón, José Z., ed., *Race, Poverty, and Social Justice: Multidisciplinary Perspectives through Service Learning*. Sterling, VA: Stylus Publishing, 2007.

Casey, Karen McKnight, Georgia Davidson, Shelley Billig, and Nicole Springer, eds. *Advancing Knowledge in Service-Learning: Research to Transform the Field*. Charlotte, NC: New Age Publishing, 2006.

Chi, Bernadette. *Service-Learning as "Citizenship Education": The Promise and the Puzzles*. Washington, DC: Corporation for National Service, 2000.

Chickering, Arthur W. *Experience and Learning: An Introduction to Experiential Learning*. New Rochelle, NY: Change Magazine Press, 1977.

Clark, Andrea Y. *Power and Service-Learning: Implications in Service-Learning for Social Justice*. Unpublished dissertation, 2009.

Coles, Robert. *The Call of Service*. Boston, MA: Houghton Mifflin, 1993.

Conderman, Bruce and Beth Patryla. "Service Learning: The Past, Present, and the Promise." *Kappa Delta Pi Record* 32, no. 4 (1996): 122–125.

Cooley, Rosa and Grace House. *School Acres: An Adventure in Rural Education*. New Haven: Yale University Press, 1930.

Cooper, David D. "Reading, Writing, and Reflection." *New Directions for Teaching and Learning* 73 (Spring 1998): 49–56.

Corporation for National Service. www.cns.gov/learn.

Counts, George S. *Dare the School Build a New Social Order?* Carbondale, IL: Southern Illinois University Press, 1978 [1932].

Coursault, Jesse. *The Learning Process*. New York: Teachers College, Columbia University, 1907.

Cunningham, Marilynn. "Assessment: An Integral Part of Experience and Learning." In *Critical Issues in K–12 Service Learning: Case Studies and Reflections*, Gita Gulati-Partee and William R. Finger, eds., 173-181. Alexandria, VA: National Society for Experiential Education, 1996.

Dewey, John. *Art as Experience. John Dewey: The Later Works, 1925-1953,* vol. 10, edited by Jo Ann Boydston (Carbondale, Illinois: Southern Illinois University Press): p.199

————. *Democracy and Education.* New York: Macmillan, 1944 [1916].

————. *Experience and Education.* New York: Macmillan, 1938.

————. *How We Think.* Mineola, NY: Dover, 1997 [1910]).

————. *How We Think: A Restatement of the Relation of Reflective Thinking to the Educative Process.* Boston: D.C. Heath and Company, 1933.

————. *Individualism Old and New.* Amherst, NY: Prometheus, 1999 [1930].

————. *Lectures in the Philosophy of Education 1899.* New York: Random House, 1966.

————. "Liberalism and Social Action." In *John Dewey: The Later Works* by Jo Ann Boydston, ed., 5–65. Carbondale, IL: Southern Illinois University Press, 1935.

————. *Reconstruction in Philosophy.* Boston, MA: The Beacon Press, 1958 [1920].

————. *The School and Society.* Carbondale, IL: Southern Illinois University Press, 1976 [1900].

————. *The Way Out of Educational Confusion.* Westport, CT: Greenwood Press, 1931.

Doherty, Austin, Marcia Mentkowski, and Kelley Conrad. "Toward a Theory of Undergraduate Experiential Learning." *New Directions for Experiential Learning* 1 (Spring 1979): 15– 26.

Donaldson, George W. and Richard Vinson. "William James, Philosophical Father of Experience-Based Education: 'The Knower Is an Actor.'" *The Journal of Experiential Education* (Fall 1979): 7–8.

Duley, James. "Field Experience Education." In *The Modern American College*, Arthur Chickering, ed. San Francisco, CA: Jossey-Bass, 1981.

Eberly, Donald. *National Service: A Promise to Keep*. Rochester, NY: J. Alden Books, 1988.

Etzioni, Amitai. *Spirit of Community*. New York: Crown Publishers, 1993.

Eyler, Janet. "Creating Your Reflection Map." *New Directions for Higher Education* 114 (Summer 2001): 35–42.

Eyler, Janet, Dwight Giles Jr., and Angela Schmiede. *A Practitioner's Guide to Reflection in Service-Learning*. Nashville TN: Vanderbilt University, 1996.

Eyler, Janet, Dwight E. Giles, Jr., Christine M. Stenson, and Charlene J. Gray. *At a Glance: What We Know about the Effects of Service-Learning on College Students, Faculty, Institutions and Communities, 1993–2000*, 3rd ed. Nashville, TN: Vanderbilt University, 2001.

Eyler, Janet and Shelley Billig, eds. *Deconstructing Service-Learning: Research Exploring Context, Participation, and Impacts*. Charlotte, NC: New Age Publishing, 2003.

Falk, Diana. "Preflection: A Strategy for Enhancing Reflection." *NSEE Quarterly* 13 (Winter 1995): 21–23.

Feuer, Lewis. "American Philosophy Is Dead." In *What Is Philosophy of Education?*, Christopher Lucas, ed., 21–35. London: Macmillan, 1969.

Fry, Ronald and David Kolb. "Experiential Learning Theory and Learning Experiences in Liberal Arts Education." *New Directions for Experiential Learning* 6 (Fall 1979): 79–92.

Ghaye, Anthony and Kay Ghaye. *Teaching and Learning through Critical Reflective Practice* (London: David Fulton Publishers, 1988).

Giarelli, James and Joseph J. Chambliss. "Philosophy of Education as Qualitative Inquiry." In *Qualitative Research in Education: Focus and Methods*, Robert R. Sherman and Rodman Webb, eds., 33–37. Philadelphia: Falmer Press, 1988.

Giles, Dwight and Janet Eyler. "The Theoretical Roots of Service-Learning in John Dewey: Toward a Theory of Service-Learning." *Michigan Journal of Community Service Learning* 1 (Fall 1994): 77–85.

Giles, Dwight, Ellen Porter Honnet, and Sally Migliore, eds.*Research Agenda for Combining Service and Learning in the 1990s*. Raleigh, NC: National Society for Internships and Experiential Education, 1991.

Gutmann, Amy. *Democratic Education*. Princeton, NJ: Princeton University Press, 1987.

Hanna, Paul. *Youth Serves the Community*. New York: D. Appleton-Century Company, 1936.

Harkavy, Ira and Lee Benson. "De-Platonizing and Democratizing Education as the Bases of Service Learning." *New Directions For Teaching and Learning* 73 (Spring 1998): 3–12.

Henderson, Harold and Stephen Hyre. "Contract Learning." *New Directions for Experiential Learning* 6 (Fall 1979): 65–78.

Hepburn, Mary. "Service Learning in Civic Education: A Concept with Long, Sturdy Roots." *Theory into Practice* 36, no. 3 (1997): 136–142.

Hesser, Garry. "Outcomes Attributed to Service-Learning and Evidence of Changes in Faculty Attitudes about Experiential Education." *Advances in Education Research* 3 (Fall 1998): 50–58.

Hewitt, Randall R. *Dewey and Power: Renewing our Democratic Faith*. Rotterdam, Netherlands: Sense, 2006.

Heybach, Jessica."Rescuing Social Justice in Education: A Critique of the NCATE Controversy." *Philosophical Studies in Education* (2009): 234–245.

Hill, Don. "Death of a Dream: Service Learning 1994–2010: An Historical Analysis by One of the Dreamers." Service Learning 2000 Center, Stanford University, 1997.

Hiott, Beverly C., W. Jackson Lyday, and H. Larry Winecoff. *Service Learning Handbook for Teacher Educators and Practitioners*. Columbia, SC: University of South Carolina.

Hocking, William. *Types of Philosophy*. New York: Scribner and Sons, 1929.

Honnet, Ellen Porter and Susan J. Poulsen. *Principles of Good Practice in Combining Service and Learning*. Racine, WI: Johnson Foundation, 1989.

Hook, Sidney. "Does Philosophy Have a Future?" In *What Is Philosophy of Education?*, Christopher Lucas, ed. London: Macmillan, 1969.

Hopkins, Richard L. *Narrative Schooling: Experiential Learning and the Transformation of American Education*. New York: Teachers College, Columbia University, 1994.

Howard, Jeffrey. "Academic Service Learning: A Counternormative Pedagogy." *New Directions for Teaching and Learning* 73 (Spring1998): 17–25.

————, ed. *Michigan Journal of Community Service Learning: Special Issue 2001: Strategic Directions for Service-Learning Research* (2001).

James, William. *Essays in Pragmatism*. New York: Hafner Press, 1948.

————. "The Moral Equivalent of War."*International Conciliation No. 2*. New York: Carnegie Endowment for International Peace, 1910.

————. *Pragmatism and the Meaning of Truth*. Cambridge, MA: Harvard University Press, 1975 [1906–7].

————. *Psychology: The Briefer Course*. Notre Dame, IN: University of Notre Dame, 1985 [1892].

Johnson, Roberta Ann and Robert C. Cope. "Social Justice and Public Policy." In *Race, Poverty, and Social Justice* by José Z. Calderón, ed., 111–122. Sterling, VA: Stylus, 2007.

Kant, Immanuel. *Critique of Pure Reason*, Paul Guyer and Allen W. Wood, eds. Cambridge, MA: Cambridge University Press, 1998 [1781].

Kellogg, Paul. Foreword to *School Acres: An Adventure in Rural Education* by Rosa Cooley and Grace House. New Haven: Yale University Press, 1930.

Kendall, Jane."Combining Service and Learning: An Introduction." In *Combining Service and Learning: A Resource Book for Community and Public Service*, Jane C. Kendall, ed., 1–33. Raleigh, NC: National Society for Internships and Experiential Education, 1990.

Kidder, Tracy. *Old Friends*. Boston: Houghton Mifflin, 1993.

Kilpatrick, William Heard. Introduction to *Youth Serves the Community* by Paul Hanna. New York: D. Appleton-Century, 1936.

————. *Philosophy of Education.* New York: Macmillan, 1951.

————. *The Project Method: The Use of the Purposeful Act in the Educative Process.* New York: Teachers College, Columbia University, 1922.

Kolb, David. *Experiential Learning: Experience as the Source of Learning and Development.* Englewood Cliffs, NJ: Prentice-Hall, 1984.

Kraft, Richard. "Service Learning: An Introduction to Its Theory, Practice, and Effects." *Advances in Education Research* 3 (Fall 1998): 7–23.

Kristeva, Julia. *Desire in Language.* New York: Columbia University Press, 1980.

Kuhn, Thomas S. *The Structure of Scientific Revolutions.* Chicago: University of Chicago Press, 1962.

Langer, Susanne. "On the Relations between Philosophy and Education." *Harvard Educational Review* 26 (Spring 1956): 139–141.

Learn and Serve Florida. *2002 Request for Proposals.*

Lipset, Seymour Jr. *American Exceptionalism.* New York: W.W. Norton, 1997.

Lisman, C. David. *Toward a Civil Society.* Westport, CT: Greenwood Publishing, 1980.

Liu, Goodwin. Introduction to *Service-Learning: A Movement's Pioneers Reflect on Its Origins, Practice, and Future*, Timothy Stanton, Dwight Giles, and Nadinne Cruz, eds.. San Francisco: Jossey-Bass, 1999.

MacIntyre, Alasdair. *After Virtue.* Notre Dame, IN: University of Notre Dame Press, 1984.

MacLeod, Jay. *Ain't No Makin' It: Aspirations and Attainment in a Low-Income Neighborhood.* Boulder, CO: Westview Press, 1987.

Mann, Horace. *Twelfth Annual Report Covering the Year 1848.* Boston, MA: Dutton and Wentworth, State Printers, 1849.

Marcuse, Herbert. *Eros and Civilization: A Philosophical Inquiry into Freud.* Boston: Beacon Press, 1955.

———. *Essay on Liberation.* Boston: Beacon Press, 1969.

———. *One-Dimensional Man: Studies in the Ideology of Advanced Industrialized Society.* Boston: Beacon Press, 1964.

Maybach, C.E. *Second-Year Evaluation of Three Components of Colorado Campus Compact.* Denver, CO: Colorado Campus Compact, 1994.

McKnight Casey, Karen, Georgia Davidson, Shelley H. Billig, Nicole C. Springer, eds. *Advancing Knowledge in Service-Learning: Research to Transform the Field.* Charlotte, NC: New Age Publishing, 2006.

McLaren, Peter. *Life in Schools: An Introduction to Critical Pedagogy in the Foundations of Education.* New York, NY: Addison Wesley Longman, 1998.

Mead, George Herbert. *Mind, Self, and Society from the Standpoint of a Social Behaviorist.* Chicago: University of Chicago Press, 1934.

Merrill, Perry Henry. *Roosevelt's Forest Army: A History of the Civilian Conservation Corps, 1933–1942.* Montpelier, VT: P.H. Merrill, 1981.

Mezirow, Jack and Associates. *Fostering Critical Reflection in Adulthood.* San Francisco: Jossey-Bass, 1990.

Millard, Richard Jr. and Peter A. Bertocci. "Philosophy and Philosophy of Education." *Journal of Education* 141 (October1958): 7–13.

Mintz, Suzanne D. and Garry Hesser."Principles of Good Practice in Service-Learning." In *Service Learning in Higher Education: Concepts and Practices*, Barbara Jacoby, ed. San Francisco: Jossey-Bass, 1997.

Mitchell, Tania. "Traditional vs. Critical Service-Learning: Engaging the Literature to Differentiate Two Models." *Michigan Journal of Community Service Learning* (2008): 50–65.

Moore, David Thornton."Experiential Education as Critical Discourse." In *Combining Service and Learning: A Resource Book for Community and Public Service*, Jane C. Kendall, ed., 273–283. Raleigh, NC: National Society for Internships and Experiential Education, 1990.

New Orleans Free School Documentary. www.educationrevolution. org/nofreeschool.html.

Noddings, Nel. *Caring*. Berkeley, CA: University of California Press, 1984.

————. *Educating for Intelligent Belief or Unbelief*. New York: Teachers College Press, 1993.

O'Connell, Brian. *Philanthropy in Action*. New York: Foundation Center, 1987.

O'Connell, William R. "Service–Learning as a Strategy for Innovation in Undergraduate Instruction." In *Service-Learning in the South: Higher Education and Public Service 1967 –1972*, William R. O'Connell ed., 1–6. Atlanta, GA: Southern Regional Education Board, 1973.

Ohio State University. service-learning.osu.edu/history.php.

O'Neil, Edward H. "The Liberal Tradition of Civic Education." In *Combining Service and Learning: A Resource Book for Community and Public Service*, Jane C. Kendall, ed., 190–200. Raleigh, NC: National Society for Internships and Experiential Education.

Payton, Robert. *Philanthropy: Voluntary Action for the Public Good.* New York: Macmillan, 1988.

Perkinson, Henry J. *The Imperfect Panacea: American Faith in Education, 1865–1965.* New York: Random House, 1968.

Points of Light Foundation. *Agencies + Schools = Service Learning: A Training Toolbox.* Washington, DC: Points of Light Foundation, 1997.

Pollock, Seth. *Three Decades of Service-Learning in Higher Education (1966–1996): The Contested Emergence of an Organizational Field.* Stanford, CA: Stanford University Press, 1997.

Putnam, Robert D. *Bowling Alone: The Collapse and Revival of American Community.* NY, New York: Simon & Schuster, 2000.

Radest, Howard. *Community Service: Encounter with Strangers.* Westport, CT: Praeger, 1993.

Rhoads, Robert. *Community Service and Higher Learning: Explorations of the Caring Self.* Albany, NY: State University of New York Press, 1997.

Root, Susan, Shelley H. Billig, and Jane Callahan, eds. *Improving Service-Learning Practice: Research on Models to Enhance Impacts.* Charlotte, NC: New Age Publishing, 2005.

Rorty, Richard. *Contingency, Irony, and Solidarity.* Cambridge, NY: Cambridge University Press, 1989.

———. "Philosophy in America Today." *The American Scholar, 51* (2), (1982): 183–200.

Schall, Keith, ed. *Stony the Road: Chapters in the History of Hampton Institute.* Charlottesville, VA: University Press of Virginia, 1977.

Seeskin, Kenneth R. "Never Speculate, Never Explain: The State of Contemporary Philosophy." *The American Scholar* 49, no. 1(1980): 19–33.

Sheffield, Eric C. "Beyond Abstraction: Philosophy as a Practical Qualitative Research Method." *The Qualitative Report* 9, no. 4 (2004): 760–769.

——. "Philosophical (Re)thinking Described and Applied." *Philosophical Studies in Education*, 36 (2005): 115–123.

——. "Root Metaphors, Paradigm Shifts, and Democratically Shared Values: Community Service-Learning as a Bridge-Building Endeavor." *Philosophical Studies in Education* (2007): 105–118.

Sherman, Robert R. Course Handout. 1995.

——. "Philosophy with Guts." *Journal of Thought* 20, no. 2 (Summer 1985): 3–11.

Shumer, Robert. "Describing Service-Learning: A Delphi Study." University of Minnesota Library, July 1993.

Sigmon, Robert. "Service-Learning: Three Principles." *Synergist* (Spring 1979): 9–11.

Silcox, Harry. *A How to Guide to Reflection: Adding Cognitive Learning to Community Service Programs.* Philadelphia, PA: Brighton Press, 1993.

Stanton, Timothy, Dwight Giles Jr.,and Nadinne Cruz, eds.. *Service-Learning: A Movement's Pioneers Reflect on Its Origins, Practice, and Future.* San Francisco: Jossey-Bass, 1999.

Stanton, Timothy. "Liberal Arts, Experiential Learning and Public Service: Necessary Ingredients for Socially Responsible Undergraduate Education." In *Combining Service and Learning: A Resource Book for Community and Public Service*, Jane Kendall, ed. Raleigh, NC: National Society for Internships and Experiential Education, 175–189.

Stanton, Timothy. "Service Learning: Groping toward a Definition." In *Combining Service and Learning*, Jane C. Kendall ed., 65–67. Raleigh, NC: National Society for Internships and Experiential Education, 1990.

Taylor, Charles. *The Ethics of Authenticity*. Cambridge, MA: Harvard University Press, 1991.

Thayer-Bacon, Barbara. "Beyond Liberal Democracy: Dewey's Renascent Liberalism." *Education and Culture* 22, no. 2 (2006): 1930.

Theobald, Paul. *Teaching the Commons*. Boulder, CO: Westview Press, 1997.

Titus, Harold. "Philosophy and the Contemporary Scene." In *What Is Philosophy of Education?*, Christopher Lucas, ed., 22–26. London: Macmillan, 1969.

Tocqueville, Alexis de. *Democracy in America*. New York: New American Library, 1956 [1835].

Toole, James and Pamela Toole. "Reflection as a Tool for Turning Service Experiences into Learning Experiences." In *Enriching the Curriculum through Service Learning*, James Tool, ed. San Francisco: Jossey-Bass, 1995.

Toulmin, Stephen. "The Recovery of Practical Philosophy." *The American Scholar*, 57, no. 3 (1988): 337–352.

Wade, Rahima. *Community Service Learning*. New York: State University of New York Press, 1997.

Weber, Max. *The Protestant Ethic and The Spirit of Capitalism* New York: Charles Scribner's Sons, 1904/1958.

West, Cornel. *Democracy Matters: Winning the Fight Against Imperialism*. New York: Penguin, 2005.

Westheimer, Joel and Jeff Kahne. "What Kind of Citizen? The Politics of Educating for Democracy." *American Educational Research Journal* 41, no. 2 (Summer 2004): 237–269.

Whitaker, Patrick. *Managing to Learn: Aspects of Reflective and Experiential Learning in Schools*. New York: Cassell, 1995.

Whitehead, Alfred North. *The Aims of Education and Other Essays*. New York: Macmillan, 1929.

Zilversmit, Arthur. *Changing Schools*. Chicago: University of Chicago Press, 1993.

Index

Parks, Rosa, *66*
Payton, Robert, *73*
Peace Corps, *30*
Peirce, C.S., *7, 20*
Penn Normal School, *21, 22, 23, 56, 69*
Pennsylvania Institute for Environmental and Community Service Learning, *120*
Perkins, Henry, *42*
philanthropy, *72, 73, 74, 75, 77, 80*
Phillips, Mindy, *35*
Points of Light Foundation, *33*
positive liberty, *57*
pragmatic, *5, 7, 12, 20, 23, 24, 26, 33, 51, 62, 64, 65, 66, 67, 91, 94, 95, 137, 140*
pragmatism, *xv, 7, 8, 23, 25, 38, 93, 95, 139*
Pragmatism, *xiii, 162*
preflection, *116, 117, 118*
progressive, *4, 8, 20, 22, 23, 24, 25, 26, 28, 29, 32, 33, 36, 45, 47, 56, 57, 63, 69, 86, 95, 102, 103, 130*
Progressive Education Association, *26, 27, 29, 101*
project method, *25, 26, 100*
Project Method, *25*
punishment, *72, 73, 76, 77*
purposeful act, *25, 100*
Putnam, Robert, *89, 90, 151*
Radest, Hpward, *72, 77, 78, 80, 81, 82, 83, 84, 85, 88, 90, 136*
Reagan, Ronald, *32*
reciprocity, *78, 79, 83*

reconstruction, *8, 39, 53, 74, 93, 101, 113, 115, 116, 120, 121, 139, 143, 145, 147*
reform, *x, 19, 26, 30, 31, 32, 39, 54, 57, 60, 124, 125*
revolution, *57, 60, 125*
Rhoads, Robert, *38, 79, 90, 160*
Rorty, Richard, *14, 82, 162*
rugged individual, *64, 65, 66, 147*
SECS, *2, 3*
Seeskin, Kenneth, *14, 162*
Service Corps Of Retired Executives, *30*
Sherman, Robert R., *xv, 12, 13, 63, 113, 162*
Shumer, Robert, *16, 17, 162*
Smith, Mr., *151, 152*
Social Construction of Knowledge, *141*
social justice, *36, 37, 38, 138, 139, 140, 145, 146, 161*
social practice, *1, 8, 9, 10, 12, 14, 52, 97*
social reproduction, *79, 131, 132, 133, 134, 144*
social-justice, *36, 37, 57, 146, 147, 155*
socially active, *2, 131, 132, 133, 136*
solidarity, *80, 82, 83, 85, 86, 88, 89, 99, 105*
Southern Regional Education Board, *30*
Stanton, Timothy, *15, 35, 162*
strong CSL, *x, 1, 2, 5, 7, 21, 34, 35, 36, 37, 39, 44, 45, 49, 50, 52, 54, 57, 64, 68, 115, 125, 126, 133, 136,*